Between Time and Eternity

The Essentials of Judaism

Jacob Neusner

Brown University

Wadsworth Publishing Company
A Division of Wadsworth, Inc.
Belmont, California

ISBN 0-8221-0160-2

ISBN-0-8221-0160-2
Library of Congress Catalog Card Number: 75-8124

Printed in the United States of America

Printing (last digit): 9 8 7 6 5

Artwork rendered for publication by Tom Martin, from drawings by Suzanne Richter Neusner.

For
Sanford Kroll
in friendship and admiration

Contents

Preface

Between Time and Eternity: The Essentials of Judaism goes over some of the subjects treated in my *Way of Torah: An Introduction to Judaism*. It is important, therefore, to explain the difference in approach and purpose between the two textbooks.

The primary theme of *Way of Torah* is that of definition. Surveying the immense varieties of Jewish belief and behavior in the modern world — from wholly secular to deeply religious and classical — we have to ask, How shall we define "Judaism"? In what way, in particular, do the inchoate phenomena called "Jewish" known in contemporary life relate to the clearly defined religious tradition of Rabbinic Judaism? In *Way of Torah*, therefore, we first describe the primary mythic structures and typological expressions of Rabbinic Judaism. We then turn to the phenomena of modern Jewish culture, the persistence of the rabbinic tradition in old forms, the development of new forms of Judaism and expressions of Jewishness. Referring in particular to these new forms, we ask how they relate to the old and how we are to interpret the new. *Way of Torah*, therefore, is a textbook meant to focus upon a fairly complex problem in the interpretation of modern and contemporary religiosity, on the one side, and on the definition of a religion in its classic and contemporary forms, on the other. It is a textbook to serve courses in which the primary problem is not the study of a particular religion but of the phenomena of religion in general.

The present work, by contrast, takes as its problem not the *comparison* of Judaism, neither the comparison of classical and modern expressions of Judaism, nor the comparison of Judaism and other religions. Rather, the problem of this book is: How can someone who knows nothing about Judaism understand the fundamental facts of Judaism? For that purpose, it seemed to me the best approach was to seize upon a considerable human dilemma, one that confronts both individuals in everyday life, and nations or societies in historical perspective. Specifically, I looked into the history of Judaism for what seemed to be the central and organizing, all-encompassing issue. My conviction is that, since the Jews are human beings, what characterizes their ongoing life is apt to express, in an idiomatic and particular way to be sure, a universal human problem, a trait of the human condition. The long history of Judaism reveals, in vast and transcendent ways, what is truly a continuing and universal tension in the life of individuals and nations: the tension between the private and the here and now, with its continuity but its boredom, and the public, historical, and collective, with its movement, change, fascination, but also its danger and disruptiveness. Intending, therefore, to introduce Judaism in particular, I could find no better way than to reach out to the condition of humankind in general.

The two, therefore, are very different from one another, even though use is made here of sections of *Way of Torah. Between Time and Eternity*, as is clear, describes the formation of Judaism in the classical, or rabbinic, formulation predominant since the first century, the primary expressions of that Judaism, and the new Reform and Zionist movements which, in the nineteenth and twentieth centuries, challenged the fundamental convictions of that Judaism. While this textbook describes Judaism in all its distinctiveness and particularity, it does so in a way which should serve students of comparative religions, in particular by introducing questions pertinent to the study of any religious tradition. But, self-evidently, the particular issues of *Way of Torah* — issues of definition and interpretation — are set aside in favor of a different set of questions,

questions about the human condition and one's philosophy of life.

Between Time and Eternity is in three chapters. In the first I outline the circumstances under which Rabbinic Judaism took shape. In the second I describe the most important traits of Rabbinic Judaism, its conception of the good life, an example of its literature, and its mythic and theological conceptions. In the final chapter I present the two great messianic movements of the modern age, and at the close offer a personal opinion on what lies before us.

My anthology, *The Life of Torah: Readings in the Jewish Religious Experience* (Encino, California, and Belmont, California, 1974: Dickenson Publishing Company, Inc.) may be read in conjunction with the present textbook, in the following way: along with the first chapter, *Life of Torah*, pp. 61-80; along with the second chapter, *Life of Torah*, pp. 17-60, 81-154; and along with the third chapter, *Life of Torah*, pp. 155-234.

In the course of the exposition, I refer to many unfamiliar words, individuals, and events. In order to make things clear, I have provided a glossary at the end, in which are listed all items not immediately familiar, together with definitions and explanations. The glossary, furthermore, includes the names of Jewish holidays and rites, important books, and other facts apt to be important in studying about Judaism. It is meant as a very small dictionary of Judaism, as well as a way of assuring that the reader has all the facts needed to understand the story which unfolds here. Extensive quotations from primary sources are included throughout the book, including talmudic discussions, important prayers, and writings of illustrative thinkers. This helps the students not only to study about Judaism but to confront some of its fundamental documents and representative figures.

My thanks go to Professor William Scott Green, University of Rochester; and Professor Robert Michaelson, University of California, for critical comments on the manuscript. My student, Rabbi Richard Sarason, kindly helped with the proofreading and pointed out valuable improvements in addition. The editorial and production staff of Dickenson Publishing Company have served me faithfully and conscientiously. I am especially grateful for all they have done to make this what I believe to be a good and useful book. The main theses of this work were presented as the Merrick Lectures at Ohio Wesleyan University in January, 1975. I appreciate the hospitality and thoughtful attention of the administration and faculty.

Jacob Neusner

Acknowledgments

The author is indebted to the following for permission to reprint copyrighted material:

The Jewish Publication Society of America for permission to quote from an introduction by Shalom Spiegel to *Legends of the Bible*, by Louis Ginzberg, © 1956, Jewish Publication Society of America.

Arthur Hertzberg for permission to include excerpts from *The Zionist Idea*, Herzl Press, © 1959 by Arthur Hertzberg.

Richard L. Rubenstein for permission to include excerpts from *After Auschwitz, Radical Theology and Contemporary Judaism*, The Bobbs-Merrill Co. Inc., © 1966 by Richard L. Rubenstein.

The American Jewish Congress for permission to quote from "Faith and the Holocaust" by Michael Wyschogrod, in *Judaism*, summer, 1971. © 1971 by American Jewish Congress.

The Union of American Hebrew Congregations for permission to include excerpts from "Putting Holiness into Words: The Mishnah and Its Laws" by Jacob Neusner, in *Keeping Posted*, Vol. XX, No. 4, January, 1975. © 1975 by the Union of American Hebrew Congregations.

The Rabbinical Assembly for permission to reprint all liturgies of Jewish worship quoted herein. Liturgies reprinted from *A Rabbi's Manual*, ed. Rabbi Jules Harlow, © 1965; *Weekday Prayer Book*, ed. Prayerbook Committee of the Rabbinical Assembly, Rabbi Gershon Hadas, chairman, and Rabbi Jules Harlow, secretary, © 1962; and *Mahzor for Rosh Hashana and Yom Kippur*, ed. Rabbi Jules Harlow, © 1972.

Introduction

The tension between two continuing, extreme interpretations of historical events determines the organization of *Between Time and Eternity*.

One view is that the great happenings of the day require close attention, are heavy with meaning. We have therefore to center our interest in the lively, important news of the day. The consequence of this approach to life, in the history of Judaism, is a yearning for the end of time, the conclusion of history, and the coming of the Messiah.

The other view is that what people should attend to is the everyday life of the home and the village, which, after all, they can do much to shape. History is something to be endured; it cannot be affected. Life at home goes on and on through time. It is, in its way, timeless, a kind of eternity. The cycle of life, birth, maturing, marriage, child-bearing, old age, and death, and the succession of days and weeks, months and seasons, year by year — these recurring patterns form a kind of eternity. And it is that timeless world of sunset, sunrise which is to be shaped and reformed.

Both views of the meaning of life and of events flourish in the history of Judaism. The former — the messianic — focuses peoples' attention upon the large and important side of life; the latter — which, as we shall see, is shaped by the rabbis of the

1

Talmud and therefore called rabbinic — stresses the timeless reality of home and hearth. The messianic mode of Judaism is not unfamiliar, particularly to people knowledgeable in the early history of Christianity. The failure of Messianism and political zealotry for that large mass of Jews that did not become Christians generated the beginning of Rabbinic Judaism.

From the second to the nineteenth century Rabbinic Judaism, with its nonhistorical and timeless emphases, tended to predominate, though important messianic movements took shape during that long period. The recent history of Judaism, in the nineteenth and twentieth centuries, by contrast, is the product of the rise of a new messianic fervor which took two important forms. One, which was optimistic, was Reform Judaism. The other, dubious about the possibilities of Jewish integration into the life of Western Europe, and fearful of the racial anti-Semitism which accompanied the emancipation of Jewry and the provision of political rights for the Jews, was Zionism.

Both Reform Judaism and Zionism have, I think, exhausted their message to Jewry. Both have said in essence everything they have to say. Their messianic message has been found wanting. Why? Because neither realized its messianic promise: Life goes on as before. Judaism of the last third of the twentieth century, like Judaism in the last third of the first century, proves remarkably ripe for the renaissance of rabbinic concern with the timeless and the enduring, as against the world-historical, the world-shaking, and world-shaping.

It is within this interpretive framework that I offer a comprehensive account of Judaism. I believe the facts and data that fill in the structure herein outlined will prove interesting for their own sake. But at the same time, they will show how the larger issues inherent in the history of Judaism work themselves out in concrete ways.

If this framework is useful, however, it will be in helping students penetrate into the human issues, the universal concerns expressed in a distinctive idiom inherent in Judaism. That is why I have outlined what I conceive to be the enduring alternatives, the permanent choices, made within Judaism. No one familiar with the history and character of American civilization will find unfamiliar the choice between a messianic conception of public life, and stress upon the ongoing, everyday mode of private being. It is when the fervor and hope of Messianism come to disappointment, when enthusiasm dies and commonplace reality intrudes, that the distinctive conceptions of Rabbinic Judaism will prove relevant and interesting. But that is for the student to discover.

Chapter One
The Foundations
of Judaism

What Do People Think Judaism Is?

Speaking of a Jewish cabinet officer, a high American government official said, "He is of the faith of the Old Testament."

Three common mistakes are contained in that single, simple, commonplace description of the Jew.

First, it is assumed that because a person is a Jew, he or she believes in the Jewish religion.

Second, it is taken for granted that the Jews call the biblical books from Genesis to Malachi "the Old Testament."

Third, and most seriously, it is imagined that the Jewish religion may be located and defined solely and entirely by opening the pages of the "Old Testament."

Let us rapidly correct the first error. For good or ill, it is an error to assume all Jews are "Judaists" — that is, people who follow the religion of Judaism. If you know Jews, who live in all fifty United States, every Canadian province, and throughout the world, you already know that it is wrong to assume all Jews believe in the Jewish religion and are Judaists. The fact is that a great many Jews, loyal to their people and faithful, according to their understanding, to what "being Jewish" requires of them, in no way participate in Judaism. They do not share its world view. They may not even know that Judaism presents a conception of the world, an interpretation of history and philosophy of life. Some of these Jews may be atheists; many may be simply indifferent to Judaism, about which they know very little. Many nonetheless continue to regard themselves as "good Jews" and to be regarded by others in the same way. Yet the religious vision of life taught by Judaism is alien — a strange, yet distinctively modern, paradox.

If our problem were to account for the modern condition of the Jewish people, then we should have to spend much time asking why large numbers of Jews are not Judaists, that is, followers of Judaism. Let us take a moment to dwell on that fact and its implications for our study. The sociology and culture of the Jews draw our attention to the decline of religiosity in all its forms. At the same time we should want to know what elements of Judaism persist in new and secular language. We want to know about *Judaism*, a religious tradition. While the facts of sociology are relevant, they are hardly central and compelling.

For a religion has to be studied as such — as a *religious* phenomenon, in and of itself — and not solely or primarily as a cultural or social force. And when we study about a religion, we study about those people who live — who view reality — within the religious world view, whose conception of life is shaped by that world view. We are not going to ask about people whose ancestors shared that world view but who themselves do not. A religious tradition has its own integrity. It may affect larger or smaller numbers of people, but that is not relevant to its description and interpretation. What is relevant is what that religion means to the people who live by it, not what it does not mean to those who do not, let alone what it does mean to those who do not.

Jews who are not Judaists therefore are not our problem. To be sure, many men and women in the modern West do not believe in God and are in no way religious. That is so for Jews, Christians, and others. It is a quite separate issue and presents an entirely self-contained problem of description and interpretation. The demise, among some, of religious belief is called secularization. To the study of modern and contemporary secularization, the Jews have much to contribute, just as much is to be learned about the Jews as a group from the study of that most fascinating phenomenon. But the study of the secular and the study of the religious, the modes of the sacred, are not the same thing. True, they relate to one another and illuminate one another. But to do both at the same time leads to confusion and not to clarity.

So for our purposes, it suffices to say not all Jews follow the Jewish religion in any form. From this point onward, we focus upon those Jews, who were nearly all of the Jewish people before modern times, and who are still a large and important segment of the Jewish people today, who both accept and live by Judaism, and who shape the Judaism of the future: the religious sector of the Jewish people.

The second error is more substantial. Judaism is based upon the biblical books written in Hebrew and Aramaic, which Christians call "the Old Testament" and which Jews call "Tanakh." Tanakh is a word made up of three letters, T, N, and K. The T stands for *Torah*, which, in Hebrew, means revelation, and refers in particular to the Five Books of Moses, the Pentateuch, which are Genesis, Exodus, Leviticus, Numbers, and Deuteronomy. The N stands for *Nevi'im*, the Hebrew word for Prophets, and refers to the biblical books of Joshua, Judges, Samuel, Kings, Isaiah, Jeremiah, Ezekiel, and the Twelve Prophets whose writings are brief, and who therefore are called "minor." These so-called minor prophets are Hosea, Joel, Amos, Obadiah, Jonah, Micah, Nahum, Habakkuk, Zephaniah, Haggai, Zechariah, and Malachi. The K stands for *Ketuvim*, meaning writings. The books of the "sacred writings" — scriptures — are Psalms, Proverbs, Job, Song of Songs, Ruth, Lamentations, Koheleth (known in the Christian Bible as Ecclesiastes), Esther, Daniel, Ezra, Nehemiah, and Chronicles. T+N+K then are supplied with vowels, becoming Tanakh (the *kh* pronounced like the *ch* in the Scottish *loch*).

Now why does it matter that what Christians call "Old Testament" has a different name for Judaism?

The difference is important. When Christians say "Old Testament," it is because they believe there is a *"New* Testament," which completes and fulfills the old. They see the religion of ancient Israel as insufficient, referring as it does to a messiah who, by the end of the story, still has not yet come. More importantly, they understand in the life and teachings of Jesus the fulfillment of the "Old Testament" prophecies. In other words, Christianity in nearly all its forms takes over the Hebrew Scriptures and supplies them with a vast interpretation based upon the life of Jesus, whom they call Christ, or messiah. This is commonly known.

What is not widely known is that, from the first century onward, Judaism took the same view of the Hebrew Scriptures. It concurred in the view that the ancient writings of Israel contained in the Tanakh presented only part of the story. The other part, Judaism held, was contained in the other Torah — in addition to the written Torah revealed in ancient times — taught in their own day by rabbis. (We shall return to this matter in a moment.) The main point is that Judaism and Christianity agree on the sanctity of the *Old Testament* = *Tanakh*, but disagree about its meaning.

Judaism is based upon both the written Torah and a second Torah, just as Christianity is based upon the Old Testament and a second and a new "Testament" or covenant. Where do we now find this second Torah, this other (and, as we shall see, *oral*) revelation? It is found in the Mishnah, a corpus of traditions and laws written down at the end of the second century C.E.*

For the present, we may therefore summarize with the following equation:

Christianity	Judaism	
$\dfrac{\text{Old Testament}}{\text{New Testament}} =$	$\dfrac{\text{Tanakh (Written Torah)}}{\text{Mishnah (Oral Torah)}}$	$>$ Torah

What a curious equation! The parts are unequal. Almost everyone in the Western world has heard of Old Testament and New Testament. Most people know how the New Testament writers, for example, in the Gospel of Matthew, will cite the Old Testament as predicting events in the life of Jesus. But the words on the Judaic side of the equation are alien and strange. Few have heard of *Tanakh*, and very few of *Mishnah*.

That is why we begin with the observation that to describe a Jew as "of the faith of the Old Testament" is simply inaccurate. But it is meant to stress something else. Judaism is not simply the religion of people who do not believe that Jesus

*"Common Era," sometimes used by Jews in place of A.D., because of the theological significance of A.D.: *Anno Domini*, the year of the Lord.

is the messiah. It also is not the sum and substance of the opinions of everyone who is Jewish, to be decided by a public opinion poll of all such people. It is not something we know about automatically, just as we naturally know a great deal about Christianity, its festivals, religious rites and beliefs, simply by going to public school or by studying Western civilization, or watching television, going to the movies, and the like. Judaism is a religion that is present (if not in equivalently vast numbers), just as Christianity is present, in the Western world. Yet it is one of the world's least comprehended religions. Part of the reason is that most people think they know something about it, when, in fact, they know very little, and what they know is at best half true.

Much that follows is going to be alien not only to Christians and people of no religious origin but also to Jews. That makes our problem still more difficult. I have already called your attention to the presence of Jews estranged from, or at best only tenuously connected to, Judaism. And many more Jews know only what is to be gained in a smattering of Sunday School lessons or in half-remembered sermons heard on the few occasions that found them in Jewish worship. What makes this an obstacle is their sense of "having heard it all," when, in fact, they have understood very little. Many of the words they have heard or said in prayer, for example, have not attracted their close attention. Some of the things we shall consider will seem familiar, while what we shall say about them appears to be strange. If we can commence with the agreement that we are studying a strange and alien religion, that everything we shall hear is new and fresh, we can build an accurate description of Judaism.

Our purpose — yours and mine — is not to determine whether Judaism is The True Religion, or whether its teachings are uniquely those by which we should guide our lives. If we ask that very legitimate question, to be addressed, in turn, to every claim anyone makes to speak truth, we must ask it in another place. For our task is simply the objective description of Judaism and the interpretation of what is described. I do not promise to give reasons why Jews should become Judaists or why Gentiles should adopt Judaism. I promise only to lead you into a strange, foreign world, a world in which people, living their lives under much the same social and cultural circumstances in which everyone finds himself or herself, see every-

thing in their own distinctive way, to be sure, you have the right
to ask how does that way differ, and how is it similar, to the
way of living chosen by others. At the end I shall answer that
question too.

You may ask, Tell me briefly what this "Judaism" is, of
which so much has been made. I shall not evade that question,
because the answer is made available in the other — the Oral —
Torah:

One day a Gentile approached Hillel, a wise man who lived
at about the beginning of the Common Era, and asked him,
"Tell me the entire Torah while you are standing on one foot."

Hillel answered, quoting Tanakh (Lev. 19:18), *"You will
love your fellow human being as yourself."*

After citing Scripture, Hillel continued, "That is the entire
Torah. All the rest is meant to explain that simple rule."

And Hillel commanded, "Now go and learn."

The Founding of Judaism

We have already observed that Tanakh ("Old Testament")
supplies the prehistory of Christianity. It also provides the
foundations of Judaism — specifically, of the form of Judaism
that dominated from the late first century to modern times and
continues to flourish in the present age. That Judaism is called
rabbinic, because its teachers are rabbis; or talmudic, because its
teachings are contained in and authoritatively taught by the
Talmud (which we shall describe shortly); or normative, in the
sense that all other modes are declared heterodox or heretical —
a highly theological adjective; or classical, in the sense that this
mode of Judaism is deemed authoritative and of enduring
excellence — another theological adjective. In alleging that
Rabbinic Judaism begins in the first century, of course, we
ignore what Rabbinic Judaism says about itself: that it was
revealed as part of the Law when Moses received the Law from
God on Mount Sinai.

Let us, therefore, listen to the language of the Rabbinic
story of its own origins. The story is remarkably brief:

When God revealed the Torah to Moses at Mount Sinai —
that is, the events depicted in the Book of Exodus — revelation

took two forms. One is the Written Torah, which is widely known. That consisted to begin with of the Five Books of Moses. Under the inspiration of God, various other prophets, psalmists, and chroniclers added to the sacred Scriptures.

But — and this is the crucial point — Moses received a second Torah as well, separate and distinct from the first. It is called the Oral Torah, for it was not written down but handed on by word-of-mouth teaching, from master to disciple. "Moses *received* Torah from Sinai and *handed it on* to Joshua, and Joshua to the elders, the elders to the prophets, the prophets gave it to the Men of the Great Assembly . . ."[1] The language used in this report of the transmission of revelation is weighty indeed. The Hebrew word "received" (*qibbel*) means also "accept." "Hand on" in Hebrew is *massar*, give to, which produces the noun, *massoret*, which means "tradition." Notice, too, the saying is not "received *the* Torah," but simply "received Torah," revelation, there being no specification of which one, or of how many.

Before we go on, let us ask how the written version of Torah differs from the other Torah, the oral one, also believed to be revealed at Sinai. For the purposes of comparison, let us look at two creation stories.

> In the beginning, two thousand years before the heaven and the earth, seven things were created: the Torah, written with black fire on white fire and lying in the lap of God; the Divine throne, erected in the heavens . . .; Paradise on the right side of God; Hell on the left side; the Celestial Sanctuary directly in front of God, having a jewel on its altar graven with the name of the Messiah, and a Voice that cries aloud, *Return, Oh you children of men.*[2]

This creation account from classical Talmudic Judaism may come as a surprise to readers more familiar with that creation legend of Scripture which states:

> In the beginning God created the heavens and the earth. The earth was without form and void, and darkness was upon the face of the deep. The spirit of God was moving over the face of the waters. And God said, Let there be light, and there was light. (Gen. 1:1-4)

Genesis says nothing about what happened before creation. God alone is responsible for the works of creation; and what he made was heaven and earth. The Talmudic creation legend, by contrast, begins with the creation of the *Torah*, not of the world, and concludes with the powerful "Voice that cries . . . ." What is striking in the rabbinic story of creation is its mystical conception of Torah, "written with black fire on white fire and lying in the lap of God."

A second, central conception of Torah occurs in a rabbinic commentary to Genesis. Before considering the passage, let me explain what is about to happen. The rabbis of the early centuries of the Common Era would look at one scriptural passage in the light of another. They would then read the one into the other. In the passage which follows, the rabbis read Proverbs 8:30 in the light of Genesis 1:1. They take a key word in the verse in Proverbs, *amon*, meaning nursling, and they play with it, changing its vowels and reading *uman*, workman. On the word-play of *amon/uman*, nursling/workman, they build their interpretation. At the same time, they understand Proverbs to be the Torah personified. Thus the Torah speaks as a real person. What does Torah say? It says, "Then I was by him as a nursling and I was daily all delight." However, having reread the verse in Proverbs through the word-play we just noted, we understand the verse in Proverbs as follows: "I, the Torah, was by him, God, as a workman, and I was daily all delight." Having read the verse in that way, we now comment as to its meaning. What it means is that the Torah was God's tool in creating the world. God looks into the Torah and shapes reality. Torah, then, is not merely a storybook or a collection of rules. Torah is the plan, the design for the whole of reality.

This is the passage:

> *Then I was by Him, as a nursling* (amon); *and I was daily all delight* (Prov. 8:30) . . . . *'amon'* is a workman (*uman*). The Torah thus declares: "I was the working tool of the Holy One, blessed be He." In human practice, when a mortal king builds a palace, he builds it not with his own skill but with the skill of an architect. The architect moreover does not build it out of his head, but employs plans and diagrams to know how to arrange the chambers and the wicket doors. Thus God

consulted the Torah and created the world, while the Torah declares *In the beginning God created* (Gen. I, 1), *Beginning* referring to the Torah, as in the verse, *The Lord made me as the beginning of His way.* (Prov. 8:22)[3]

Now we have a much clearer picture of the rabbinic conception of Torah. It is God's plan and design for the world; it contains and reveals what God had in mind when he made the world.

These two passages in rabbinic literature alert us to a wholly new situation, a situation as remarkable, in its way, as was the early Christians' reading into ancient Scripture of the life and teachings of Jesus. "Torah" no longer means "The Five Books of Moses." It no longer seems to refer narrowly to "revelation." The *rabbinic* Torah here gains an autonomous, independent existence, a personality of its own, Oral Torah — that of the rabbis — relates (to stretch our analogy to its limits) to the Torah of Moses as the Christ of faith compares to the Jesus of history.

That is to say, Christians believe many more things about Jesus — things he said or did or taught — than historians are able to show actually happened, were really said or done by him. Similarly, "the whole Torah of Moses" including a vast corpus of teachings not contained in the written Scriptures contains much more than historians are able to locate, through normal inquiries, in the "original Torah of Moses." The "whole Torah" tells us far more than historians think we may reliably attribute to Moses' own teaching. To put it more simply, it is virtually impossible to show with certainty that any of the so-called "Five Books of Moses" derives directly or even indirectly from a historical personality of that name.

What actually happened matters: It helps us to interpret the difference between the facts of history, such as they are (and they are very few), and the fantasies of faith, or belief. But for our present purpose, it is faith which requires description and analysis. Since Judaism is a living religion, our problem is to understand what people believe, how they view reality, and not whether what they believe is verifiable by the normal procedures of historians. Truth, after all, takes many forms, and insight, though presented in the form of a story about things which happened once upon a time, contains a truth to which "once upon a time" really matters very little.

Central to Judaism as it flourished from the second century onward, therefore, is a tremendous, encompassing, reality-defining symbol. In a myriad of ways, it serves as the final referent, the evocative image, the single word which stands for and summarizes all being. It would, indeed, be more accurate to use the word "Torah" where we refer to "Judaism," for "Judaism" is an immense abstraction, an *-ism*, that is, a word which suggests a systematic body of doctrine and belief. Torah, by contrast, makes room for all of the phenomena produced within Rabbinic Judaism (and much else). To the degree that "Judaism" has a name for itself, *Torah* is that name.

And Torah means revelation. So "Judaism" is "Torah," and "Torah" is the sum and substance of what God revealed to Moses, whom the rabbis call *our rabbi*. The system is whole, complete, and self-contained, addressing itself to fundamentals.

But before we proceed to describe that system, let us return to its history. Whence this religion of Torah, the revelation of Moses *our rabbi*, the whole Torah, consisting of two parts, one written, the other accepted by Moses and handed on in the endless process of tradition?

First, we continue our consideration of the rabbinic history of "Torah," of "Judaism." The sentence about Moses' receiving Torah from Sinai brings us as far as the prophets' successors, who are called "The Men of the Great Assembly." Then the rabbis list two intervening names, Simeon the Righteous, who was "one of the remnants of the Great Assembly," and Antigonus of Sokho, who received Torah from Simeon the Righteous. Then the list breaks down into pairs, five in all: Yosé the son of Yo'ezer, and Yosé the son of Yoḥanan (Yosé is a diminutive of Yosef or Joseph, and Yoḥanan is the Hebrew form of the name John, thus: Joseph the son of John); then Joshua the son of Peraḥiah, and Nittai; then Judah the son of Tabbai, and Simeon the son of Shaṭaḥ; then Shammai and Hillel. That, in substance, is the whole chain. Hillel ends it — at the first century.

We shall not ask who these particular people were. What is important in the list is not the identity of the names on it, but the fact that specific individuals are named. What this means is that rabbinic history of Torah claims to be the history of real, live men (no women are mentioned), who, beginning with

Moses and going down to Hillel, have received and transmitted revelation. Accordingly, of central importance in Torah are the men who receive and transmit it.

These men are conceived to be disciples, then masters: teachers in a long process of learning. "Torah" is conceived to be something one can learn, then teach to others, a corpus of traditions which take the form of words and reside in the intellect. The experience made available by Torah is going to be the experience of the shaping of the mind. The message of Torah is going to concern things we think about and deeds we do as a result of consciousness, of thought.

When we stand back from the rabbinic history of Torah, however, and examine it in accord with the way historians study past events, we have to ask what the sources can tell us. And that means not only, what is the story a given source purports to report? but, how does the person who tells the story know it? If historians are not first-hand observers — and they rarely are — then what is the source behind our source? If the narrators lived long after the events narrated, then is it not likely that they project on to the past their own conception of how things had to have happened, rather than how they really were? In other words, when we study the history of a religion, we cannot be satisfied with the history provided by the authorities of that religion. We have to stand back from that history as a report of holy events and take a position outside the circle of faith.

The history of "Torah" told by the rabbis therefore has to be set aside in favor of the history of the various kinds of Judaism reported in many different sources deriving from, or speaking about, the period before the emergence of Rabbinic Judaism. Our first sure point of reference, clearly, will be the point at which we have good reason to suppose Rabbinic Judaism stood fully revealed in the light of history. That time is the first century C.E., particularly the latter third of that century.

Two Ways of Understanding History: The Alternative of Rabbinic Judaism

Rabbinic Judaism was born in the first century C.E., a time of acute crisis. It is the outcome of one among several ap-

proaches to that crisis. Its character — the reason for its remarkable endurance for more than eighteen centuries — can only be
understood when we grasp the nature of the crisis, and how it
brought about the distinctive restructuring of old conceptions
in a new way.

To begin with, however, let us stand back and consider the
great issue facing any society, not simply the Jewish society of
first century Palestine. The issue is this: How do we respond to
history, to events, to the ups and downs of life? Every group
that survives long enough experiences "history," those note-
worthy events, those ups and downs of life. The events of
individual life — birth, maturing, marriage, death — do not
make, or add up to, history, except for individuals. But the
events of group-life — formation of the group, developing social
norms and patterns, depression or prosperity, war or peace —
these do make history. When a small people coalesces and
begins its course through history in the face of adversity, two
things can happen.

Either the group disintegrates in the face of disaster, loses
its hold on its individual members.

Or the group fuses and is strengthened by trial, is able to
turn adversity into the occasion of renewal.

Obviously, the Jewish people has known the mystery of
how to endure through history, for it is one of the oldest
peoples now alive on the face of the earth. Even in the times
described by Tanakh, adversity elicited conscious and self-
conscious response. Things did not merely *happen to* the
ancient Israelites. Events were shaped, reformed, and *interpreted by* them, made into the raw materials for a renewal of
the life of the group. The reason is that the ancient Israelites
regarded their history as important and significant, as teaching
lessons. History was not merely "one damn thing after
another." It had a purpose and was moving somewhere. The
writers of Leviticus and Deuteronomy, of the historical books
from Joshua through Kings, and of the prophetic literature,
agree that when Israel does God's will, they enjoy times of
peace, security, and prosperity, and when they do not, they are
punished at the hands of mighty kingdoms, themselves raised up
as instruments of God's wrath. This conception of the meaning
of Israel's life produced a further question: How long? When do
the great events of time come to their climax and conclusion?

And in answer to that question, the hope for the Messiah, the anointed of God who would redeem the people and set them on the right path forever, thus ending the vicissitudes of history, was born.

Now, when we reach the first century C.E., we come to a turning point in the messianic hope. No one who knows the Gospels will be surprised to learn of the intense, vivid, prevailing expectation that the Messiah was coming soon. And it is hardly astonishing that that should be the case, for people who fix their attention on everyday events of world-shaking dimensions naturally will look forward to a better future.

What is surprising is the development of a second, quite different response to history. It is the response of people prepared once and for all to transcend everyday events, to take their leave of wars and rumors of wars, of politics and public life, and to attempt to construct a new reality above history, a way of viewing reality outside of the everyday life. This is not merely a craven or exhausted passivity in the face of world-shaking events. It represents — I repeat — the active construction of a new mode of being. The decision is to exercise freedom to reconstruct conceptions of the meaning and ultimate significance of what happens. It is a seeking of a world, not outside this one, but, at least, different from and better than the one formed by ordinary history. It is a quest for eternity in the here and now, an effort to form a society capable of abiding amid change and storm. Indeed, it is a fresh reading of the meaning of history: The nations of the world make history and think what they do matters. But Israel knows that it is God who makes history, and it is the reality formed in response to God's will which *is* history. It is that reality, that conception of time and change, which is the focus and the vision of Rabbinic Judaism.

Rabbinic Judaism is essentially a metahistorical approach to life. It expresses an intense inwardness, and lays its stress upon the ultimate meaning contained within small and humble affairs. Rabbinic Judaism set itself up as the alternative to all the forms of Messianic Judaism — whether leading to Christianity or to militaristic Zealotry and nationalism — that claimed to know the secret of history: the time of, and way to, redemption.

Rabbinic Judaism is the creation of the meeting of Pharisee

and Scribe before the destruction of the Second Temple of Jerusalem in the year 70 C.E.

It flows out of Pharisaism, a particular sect in ancient Palestine.

It is shaped by the convictions of the Scribes, the professional class of teachers of Torah, petty officials and bureaucrats of that same period.

The Scribes knew and taught Torah. They took their interpretation of Torah very seriously, it goes without saying, and the act of study to them was of special importance.

The Pharisees had developed, for their part, a peculiar perception of how to live and interpret life, which we may call an *as if* perception. In very specific ways, as we shall see in a moment, the Pharisees claimed to live *as if* they were priests, *as if* they had to obey the laws that applied to the Temple. When the Temple itself was destroyed, it turned out that the Pharisees had prepared for that tremendous change in the sacred economy. They continued to live as if — as if the Temple stood, as if there was a new Temple formed of the Jewish people.

Joined to their mode of looking at life was the substance of the Scribal ideal, the stress on learning of Torah and carrying out its teachings.

What brought the two components together — the one, the Pharisaic mode of *experiencing* everyday life; the other, the Scribal way of *interpreting* it through Tanakh — was the impact of the destruction of the Temple itself.

But we have moved far ahead of our story. Thus far, we have considered the emergence of Rabbinic Judaism in a most general way. We have laid out the alternatives to how great events were to be experienced and understood.

One was — and is — the historical-Messianic way, stressing the importance of those events and concentrating upon their weight and meaning.

The other was — and is — the metahistorical-Rabbinic way, laying emphasis upon the transcendence of events and the construction of an eternal, changeless mode of being, capable of riding out the waves of history.

These considerable generalizations now require the flesh of historical description. Once we have analyzed the specific texts that reveal the way in which people responded to the cataclysm represented by the destruction of the Second Temple, the generalizations just now stated will take on much more meaning.

The Destruction of the Second Temple and the Birth of Rabbinic Judaism

The destruction of the Second Temple marked the major turning point in the history of Judaism in late antiquity. The end of the cult of animal sacrifice, which from remote times had supplied a chief means of service to God, changed the ways of divine worship, since the sacrifice of animals in the Temple had formerly predominated. The loss of the building itself was of considerable consequence, for the return to Zion and the rebuilding of the Temple in the sixth and fifth centuries B.C.E. had long been taken to mean that Israel and God, supposed by prophecy to have been estranged from one another because of idolatry in First Temple times, had been reconciled. Finally, the devastation of Jerusalem, the locus of cult and Temple piety, intensified the perplexity of the day, for from ancient times the city, as much as what took place in its Temple, was holy. By August, 70 C.E., the cultic altar, the Temple and the holy city lay in ruins — a considerable calamity. What issue faced the Jews after the destruction of the Temple? It was fundamentally social and religious, not primarily a matter of government or politics.

We shall examine four responses to the challenges of the destruction of Jerusalem, the end of the Temple, and the cessation of the cult of animal sacrifice. These responses had to deal with several crucial social and religious problems, all interrelated. First, how to achieve atonement without the cult? Second, how to explain the disaster of the destruction? Third, how to cope with the new age, to devise a way of life on a new basis entirely? Fourth, how to account for the new social forms consequent upon the collapse of the old social structure? As we shall see, it was in the process of answering these questions that Rabbinic Judaism was born. Its success in responding to them guaranteed its future. At the very end of the discussion, I shall claim that the modern situation of Judaism is remarkably similar to that of the first century. Just as at that time

Messianism had played its role and run out of persuasive ideas, so today the major modes of modern Messianism in Judaism have had their say. Just as at that time attention turned, after tumultuous historical events, to the here and now, so today the everyday becomes important.

We deal with four responses to the crisis of the destruction of the Second Temple. This will help us to see early Rabbinic Judaism in the proper perspective, to understand the choices before it and the selections it made in the context of the choices made by others.

The four responses are of, first, the apocalyptic writers represented in the visions of Baruch and II Ezra; second, the Dead Sea community at Qumran; third, the Christian church; and finally, the Pharisaic sect. The apocalyptic visionaries were writers who tried to interpret the meaning of events. They expected the imminent end of time, a cosmic cataclysm in which God would destroy evil and establish righteousness. The Dead Sea community at Qumran, discovered in 1947, formed a kind of sectarian monastery, with its particular way of seeing the meaning of history. The Christian church needs no introduction. The Pharisaic sect does, however, and we shall take some trouble to explain who the Pharisees were and how we know about them.

We begin with the group most interested in the meaning of history, in the coming of the Messiah and the end of time. They were the apocalyptic visionaries, who claimed to interpret the great events of the day and to know where they were leading.

When the apocalyptic visionaries looked backward upon the ruins, they saw a tragic vision. So they emphasized future, supernatural redemption, which they believed was soon to come. The Qumranians had met the issues of 70 C.E. long before in a manner essentially similar to that of the Christians. Both groups abandoned the Temple and its cult and replaced them by means of the new community, on the one hand, and the service or pious rites of the new community, on the other. The Pharisees come somewhere between the first, and the second and third groups. Like the apocalyptics, they saw the destruction as a calamity; but like the Dead Sea sect and the Christians, they sought the means, in both social forms and religious expression, to provide a new way of atonement and a new form of divine service, to constitute a new, interim Temple.

THE APOCALYPTIC RESPONSE

Two documents, the Apocalypse of Ezra and the Vision of Baruch, are representative of the apocalyptic state of mind. The compiler of the Ezra apocalypse (2 Ezra 3-14), who lived at the end of the first century, C.E., looked forward to a day of judgment when the Messiah would destroy Rome and God would govern the world. But he had to ask, How can the suffering of Israel be reconciled with divine justice? To Israel, God's will had been revealed. But God had not removed the inclination to do evil, so men could not carry out God's will:

> For we and our fathers have passed our lives in ways that bring death ... But what is man, that thou art angry with him, or what is a corruptible race, that thou art so bitter against it? ... (Ezra 8:26)

Ezra was told that God's ways are inscrutable (4:10-11), but when he repeated the question, "Why has Israel been given over to the Gentiles as a reproach," he was given the answer characteristic of this literature — that a new age was dawning that would shed light on such perplexities. Thus, he was told:

> ... if you are alive, you will see, and if you live long, you will often marvel, because the age is hastening swiftly to its end. For it will not be able to bring the things that have been promised to the righteous in their appointed time, because this age is full of sadness and infirmities ... (4:10-26)

An angel told him the signs of the coming redemption, saying:

> ... the sun shall suddenly shine forth at night and the moon during the day, blood shall drip from wood, and the stone shall utter its voice, the peoples shall be troubled, and the stars shall fall ... (5:4-5)

And he was admonished to wait patiently:

> The righteous therefore can endure difficult circumstances, while hoping for easier ones, but those who

have done wickedly have suffered the difficult circumstances, and will *not* see easier ones. (6:55-56)

The writer thus regarded the catastrophe as the fruit of sin;
more specifically, the result of the *natural* human incapacity to
do the will of God. He prayed for forgiveness and found hope in
the coming transformation of the age and the promise of a new
day, when the human heart would be as able, as the mind even
then was willing, to do the will of God.

The pseudepigraph in the name of Jeremiah's secretary,
Baruch, likewise brought promise of coming redemption, but
with little practical advice for the intervening period. The
document exhibits three major themes.

First, God acted righteously in bringing about the punishment of Israel:

> Righteousness belongs to the Lord our God, but
> confusion of face to us and our fathers . . . (Baruch 2:6)

Second, the catastrophe came on account of Israel's sin:

> Why is it, O Israel . . . that you are in the land of your
> enemies . . . ? You have forsaken the fountain of
> wisdom. If you had walked in the way of the Lord, you
> would be dwelling in peace forever. (3:10-12)

Third, as surely as God had punished the people, so
certainly would he bring the people home to their land and
restore their fortunes. Thus Jerusalem speaks:

> But I, how can I help you? For He who brought these
> calamities upon you will deliver you from the hand of
> your enemies . . . For I sent you out with sorrow and
> weeping, but God will give you back to me with joy and
> gladness forever . . . (4:17-18, 23)

Finally, Baruch advised the people to wait patiently for
redemption, saying:

> My children, endure with patience the wrath that has
> come upon you from God. Your enemy has overtaken

you, but you will soon see their destruction and will
tread upon their necks . . . For just as you purposed to
go astray from God, return with tenfold zeal to seek
Him. For He who brought these calamities upon you
will bring you everlasting joy with your salvation. Take
courage, O Jerusalem, for He who named you will
comfort you. (4:25, 28-30)

The saddest words written in these times come in 2 Baruch:

Blessed is he who was not born, or he who, having been
  born, has died
But as for us who live, woe unto us
Because we see the afflictions of Zion and what has
  befallen Jerusalem . . . (10:6-7)
You husbandmen, sow not again.
And earth, why do you give your harvest fruits?
Keep within yourself the sweets of your sustenance.
And you, vine, why do you continue to give your wine?
For an offering will not again be made therefrom in Zion.
Nor will first-fruits again be offered.
And do you, O heavens, withhold your dew,
And open not the treasuries of rain.
And do you, sun, withhold the light of your rays,
And you, moon, extinguish the multitude of your light.
For why should light rise again
Where the light of Zion is darkened? . . . (10:9-12)
Would that you had ears, O earth,
And that you had a heart, O dust,
That you might go and announce in Sheol,
And say to the dead,
"Blessed are you more than we who live." (11:6-7)

Here we see the end of the messianic mentality, the ultimate
result of concentrating on great events. The issue before all
groups is, What to do now, today? We have suffered disaster.
What is its meaning and where are we heading? The answer of
this sad poem is utter nihilism. Once we are told, "We have no
answer but patience," the next step is going to be the end of
patience. But there is no new beginning. The apocalyptic writers
have nothing to say to those who wait but "wait some more."

No wonder then they conclude that death is better than life. For those who live, however, such a message is curiously inappropriate. Before we proceed, let us consider how a rabbi of the period responded to the nihilistic message of the disappointed Messianists.

A leading rabbi after 70, Rabbi Joshua, met such people. It was reported that when the Temple was destroyed, "ascetics multiplied in Israel," who would neither eat flesh nor drink wine. Rabbi Joshua dealt with them thus:

> He said to them, "My children, On what account do you not eat flesh and drink wine?"
>
> They said to him, "Shall we eat meat, from which they used to offer a sacrifice on the altar, and now it is no more? And shall we drink wine, which was poured out on the altar, and now it is no more?"
>
> He said to them, "If so, we ought not to eat bread, for there are no meal offerings any more. Perhaps we ought not to drink water, for the water-offerings are not brought anymore."
>
> They were silent.
>
> He said to them, "My children, come and I shall teach you. Not to mourn at all is impossible, for the evil decree has already come upon us. But to mourn too much is also impossible, for one may not promulgate a decree for the community unless most of the community can endure it . . . But thus have the sages taught: 'A man plasters his house, but leaves a little piece untouched. A man prepares all the needs of the meal, but leaves out some morsel. A woman prepares all her cosmetics, but leaves off some small item . . .' " (b. Bava Batra 60b)

The response of the visionaries is, thus, essentially negative. All they had to say is that God is just and Israel has sinned, but, in the end of time, there will be redemption. What to do in the meantime? Merely wait. Not much of an answer.

THE DEAD SEA SECT

For the Dead Sea community, the destruction of the Temple cult took place long before 70 C.E. By rejecting the

Temple and its cult of blood sacrifice, the Qumran community had had to confront a world without Jerusalem even while the city was still standing. The spiritual situation of Yavneh, the community formed by the Pharisaic rabbis after the destruction of the Temple in 70, and that of Qumran, are strikingly comparable. As the Qumran sectarians constructed a Judaism without the Temple cult, the Pharisaic rabbis also had to do so — at least temporarily. The difference, of course, is that the rabbis witnessed the destruction of the city by others, while the Qumran sectarians did not lose the Temple, but rejected it at the outset.

The founders of the Qumran community were Temple priests, who saw themselves as continuators of the true priestly line. For them the old Temple was, as it were, destroyed in the times of the Maccabees by falling into the hands of usurpers. Its cult was defiled, not by the Romans, but by the rise of a high priest from a family other than theirs. They further rejected the calendar followed in Jerusalem. They therefore set out to create a new Temple to serve until God, through the Messiah in the line of Aaron, would establish the true Temple once again. The Qumran community believed that the presence of God had left Jerusalem and had come to the Dead Sea. The *community* now constituted the new Temple, just as some elements in early Christianity saw the new Temple in the body of Christ, in the Church, the Christian community. In some measure, this represents a "spiritualization" of the old Temple, for the Temple was the community, and the Temple worship was effected through the community's study and fulfillment of the Torah. But the community was just as much a reality, a presence, as was the Jerusalem Temple; the obedience to the law was no less than the blood sacrifices. Thus, the Qumranians represent a middle point between reverence for the old Temple and its cult, and complete indifference in favor of the Christians' utter spiritualization of both, represented, for example, in the Letter to the Hebrews.

If the old Temple is destroyed, then how will Israel make atonement? The Qumranian answer is that the life of the community in perfect obedience to the Law is represented as the true sacrifice offered in the new Temple. The community thus takes over the holiness and the functions of the Temple and so is the only means of maintaining the holiness of Israel and making atonement for sin. The response of the Dead Sea sect, therefore, was to reconstruct the Temple and to reinterpret the nature and substance of sacrifice. The community constituted the reconstructed Temple. The life of Torah and obedience to its commandments formed the new sacrifice.

THE CHRISTIAN COMMUNITY

The study of the beginning of Rabbinic Judaism comprehends a considerable part of early Christian experience, simply because for a long time in Palestine, as well as in much of the Diaspora, Christians were another kind of Jew and saw themselves as such. Moreover, the Christians, whether originally Jewish or otherwise, took over the antecedent holy books and much of the ritual life of Judaism. For our purposes they serve, therefore, as another form of Judaism, one which differed from the others primarily in regarding the world as redeemed through the Word and Cross of Jesus. But one must hasten to stress the complexity of the Christian evidences. Indeed, the response of the Christians to the destruction of the Temple cannot be simplified and regarded as essentially unitary.

Because of their faith in the crucified and risen Christ, Christians experienced the end of the old cult and the old Temple before it actually took place, much like the Qumran sectarians. They had to work out the meaning of the sacrifice of Jesus on the cross, and whether the essays on that central problem were done before or after 70 C.E. is of no consequence. The issues of August, 70, when the Temple was destroyed, confronted Qumranians and Christians for other than narrowly historical reasons; for both the events of that month took place, so to speak, in other than military and political modes. But the effects were much the same. The Christians, therefore, resemble the Qumranians in having had to face the end of the cult before it actually ended. But they were like the Pharisees in having to confront the actual destruction of the Temple, then and there.

Like the Qumranians, the Christian Jews criticized the Jerusalem Temple and its cult. Both groups in common believed that the last days had begun. Both believed that God had come to dwell with them, as he had once dwelled in the Temple. The sacrifices of the Temple were replaced, therefore, by the sacrifice of a blameless life and by other spiritual deeds. But the Christians differ on one important point. To them, the final sacrifice had already taken place; the perfect priest had offered up the perfect sacrifice, his own body. So, for the Christians, Christ on the cross completed the old sanctity and inaugurated the new. This belief took shape in different ways. For Paul, in 1 Corinthians 3:16-17, the Church is the new Temple, Christ is the foundation of the "spiritual" building. Ephesians 2:18ff. has Christ as the cornerstone of the new building, the company of Christians constituting the Temple.

Perhaps the single most coherent statement of the Christian view of cult comes in Hebrews. Whether or not Hebrews is representative of many Christians or comes as early as 70 C.E. is not our concern. What is striking is that the Letter explores the great issues of 70: the issues of cult, Temple, sacrifice, priesthood, atonement, and redemption. Its author takes for granted that the Church is the Temple, that Jesus is the builder of the Temple, and that he is also the perfect priest and the final and most unblemished sacrifice. Material sacrifices might suffice for the ceremonial cleansing of an earthly sanctuary, but if sinners are to approach God in a heavenly sanctuary, a sacrifice different in kind and better in degree is required. It is Jesus who is that perfect sacrifice, who has entered the true, heavenly sanctuary and now represents his people before God: "By his death he has consecrated the new convenant together with the heavenly sanctuary itself." Therefore, no further sacrifice — his or others' — is needed.

The Christian response to the crisis of the day was both entirely appropriate and quite useless. It was appropriate for those who already shared the Christian belief that the Messiah had come and that the Temple that had been destroyed in any case no longer mattered. But this was a message of little substance for those who did not stand within the Christians' circle of faith. To them, the crisis was real, the problem intense and immediate. So far as the Christians formed a small group within the Jewish people, their explanation and interpretation of the disaster was of limited appeal. What they offered was one Messianism in place of another. It was the Messianism built upon the paradox of the crucified Messiah, the scandal of weakness in place of strength, suffering unto death in place of this-worldly victory. True, that Messianism was to speak to millions of men and women through the ages. But to people who believed the Messiah would be a great general who would throw off the rule of pagans and lead the people to an age of peace and prosperity, the Christian Messiah hanging on the cross proved to be an insufferable paradox. It was not that Christianity was irrelevant. It was that its answers could not be understood by people who were asking a different question.

THE PHARISEES BEFORE 70

We come now to the Pharisees, forerunners of Rabbinic Judaism. First we want to know about their traits before the destruction of the Temple in 70. Then we shall ask about their message in the time of ultimate crisis.

We know very little about the Pharisees before the time of Herod. During Maccabean days, according to Josephus, our sole reliable source, they appear as a political party, competing with the Sadducees, another party, for control of the court and government. Afterward, they all but fade out of Josephus's narrative. But the later rabbinical literature fills the gap and tells a great many stories about Pharisaic masters from Shammai and Hillel, at the end of the first century B.C.E., to the destruction in 70 C.E. It also ascribes numerous sayings, particularly on matters of law, both to the masters and to the Houses, or Schools, of Shammai and of Hillel. These circles of disciples seem to have flourished in the first century, down to 70 and beyond.

What was the dominant trait of Pharisaism before 70? It was, as depicted both in the later rabbinic traditions about the Pharisees and in the Gospels, concern for certain matters of rite: in particular, eating one's meals in a state of ritual purity *as if* one were a Temple priest, and carefully giving the required tithes and offerings due to the priesthood. The Gospels' stories and sayings on Pharisaism also added fasting, Sabbath-observance, affirming vows and oaths, and the like, but the main point was keeping the ritual purity laws outside of the Temple, as well as inside, where the priests had to observe ritual purity when they carried out the requirements of the cult. (To be sure, the Gospels also include a fair amount of hostile polemic, some of it rather extreme, but these polemical matters are not our concern. All one may learn from the accusations —

for instance, that the Pharisees were a brood of vipers, morally blind, sinners, and unfaithful — is one fact: Christian Jews and Pharisaic Jews were at odds.)

The Pharisees were those Jews who believed that one must keep the purity laws outside of the Temple. Other Jews, following the plain sense of Leviticus, supposed that purity laws were to be kept only in the Temple, where the priests had to enter a state of ritual purity in order to carry out the requirements of the cult, such as animal sacrifice. Priests also had to eat their Temple food in a state of ritual purity, but lay people did not. To be sure, everyone who went to the Temple had to be ritually pure. But outside the Temple the laws of ritual purity were not widely observed, for it was not required that noncultic activities be conducted in a state of Levitical cleanness.

But as I said, the Pharisees held to the contrary that even outside of the Temple, in one's own home, one had to follow the laws of ritual purity in the only circumstance in which they might apply, namely, at the table. They therefore held one must eat secular food, that is, ordinary, everyday meals, in a state of ritual purity *as if one were a Temple priest*. The Pharisees thus assumed for themselves — and therefore all Jews equally — the status and responsibilities of the Temple priests. The table in the home of every Jew was seen to be like the table of the Lord in the Jerusalem Temple. The commandment, "You shall be a kingdom of priests and a holy people," was taken literally. The whole country was considered holy. The table of every Jew possessed the same order of sanctity as the table of the cult. But, at this time, only the Pharisees held such a viewpoint, and eating unconsecrated food as if one were a Temple priest at the Lord's table thus was one of the two significations that a Jew was a Pharisee, a sectarian.

The other was meticulous tithing. The agricultural rules required giving a portion of one's crops to the priests and Levites; planting seeds in such a way that several varieties were not mixed together; not making use of the fruit of trees before the fourth year after their planting; and various other taboos. The laws of tithing, and related agricultural taboos, may have been kept primarily by Pharisees. Of this we are not certain. Pharisees clearly regarded keeping the agricultural rules as a chief religious duty. But whether, to what degree, and how other Jews did so, is not clear. Both the agricultural laws and purity rules in the end affected table-fellowship: *How and what one may eat.* That is, they were "dietary laws."

The Dead Sea sect, the Christian Jews, and the Pharisees all stressed the eating of ritual meals. But while the Qumranians and the Christians tended to oppose sacrifice as such, and to prefer to achieve forgiveness of sin through ritual baths and communion meals, the Pharisees before 70 continued to revere the Temple and its cult, and afterward they drew up the laws which would govern the Temple when it would be restored. While awaiting restoration, they held that "As long as the Temple stood, the altar atoned for Israel. But now a man's table atones for him."4

This Pharisaic attitude would be highly appropriate to the time when the Temple no longer stood. The Pharisees had already entered that time, in a strange and paradoxical way, by pretending to be Temple priests. But the pretense contained within itself the germ of a great revolution, for the real issue is the matter of the sacred. Every Jew believed in holiness, in a God who set apart a place, the Temple, for the sacred. Every Jew knew that there was a certain hocus pocus, a set of rites, that prepared one for the encounter with the sacred. What the Pharisees held before 70 was not merely the fantasy that they would act like priests. Their message before 70 was that the sacred is not limited to the Temple, that the country is holy, the people is holy, the land is holy. The life of the people, not merely the cult of the Temple, is capable of sanctification. How do priests serve God? They purify themselves and offer sacrifices. How should the holy people serve God? They should purify themselves — sanctifying themselves by ethical and moral behavior. They should offer the sacrifice of a contrite heart, as the Psalmist had said, and they should serve God through loyalty and through love, as the prophets had demanded.

In other words, the Pharisaic message to the time of crisis, in its strange and limited way, was to recover in Scripture those elements that stressed the larger means of service to God than were available in the Temple. Their method — the way of living *as if* one were a priest — contained a message to all that the Jews had left in the aftermath of the messianic war of 70 C.E.: The Temple which is left is the people. The surviving holy place is the home and the village. The cult is the life of community.

The Pharisees never opposed the Temple, though they were critical of the priesthood. While it stood, they seem to have accepted the efficacy of the cult for the atonement of sins, and in this regard, as in others, they were more loyal than other sects to what they took to be the literal meaning of Scripture. More radical groups moved far beyond that meaning, either through rejecting its continued validity, as in the Christian view, or through taking over the cult through their own commune, as in the Qumran view.

While in the early Christians gathered for ritual meals, and made them the climax of their group life, the Pharisees apparently did not. What expressed the Pharisees' sense of self-awareness as a group apparently was not a similarly intense, ritual meal. Eating was not a ritualized occasion, even though the Pharisees had liturgies to be said at the meal. No communion-ceremony, no rites centered on meals, no specification of meals on holy occasions characterize Pharisaic table-fellowship, which was a quite ordinary, everyday affair. The various fellowship-rules had to be observed in a wholly routine circumstance — daily, at every meal, without accompanying rites other than a benediction for the food. Unlike those of the Pharisees, the Christians' myths and rituals rendered table-fellowship into a much heightened spiritual experience: *Do these things in memory of me*. The Pharisees told no stories about purity laws, except (in later times) to account for their historical development (for example, who had decreed which purity-rule?). When they came to table, so far as we know, they told no stories about how Moses had done what they now did, and they did not "do these things in memory of Moses 'our rabbi.'"

In the Dead Sea commune, table-fellowship was open upon much the same basis as among the Pharisees: appropriate undertakings to keep ritual purity and to consume properly grown and tithed foods. As we know it, the Qumranian meal was liturgically not much different from the ordinary Pharisaic gathering. The rites pertained to, and derived from, the eating of food and that alone.

Both Christians and Pharisees lived among ordinary folk, while the Qumranians did not. In this respect the commonplace character of Pharisaic table-fellowship is all the more striking. The sect ordinarily did not gather *as a group* at all, but kept

their rites in the home. All meals required ritual purity.
Pharisaic table-fellowship took place in the same circumstances
as did all nonritual table-fellowship. Common folk ate everyday
meals in an everyday way, among ordinary neighbors who were
not members of the sect. They were engaged in workaday
pursuits like everyone else. The setting for law-observance was
the field and the kitchen, the bed and the street. The occasion
for observance was set every time a person picked up a nail,
which might be unclean, or purchased a *se'ah* of wheat, which
had to be tithed. There were no priests present to bless the
Pharisees' deeds or sages to instruct them. Keeping the Pharisaic
rule required neither an occasional exceptional rite at, but
external to, the meal, as in the Christian sect, nor taking up
residence in a monastic commune, as in the Qumranian sect.
Instead, it imposed the perpetual ritualization of daily life, on
the one side, and the constant, inner awareness of the
communal order of being, on the other.

THE PHARISEES AFTER 70

The response of the Pharisees to the destruction of the
Temple is known to us only from rabbinic materials, which
underwent revisions over many centuries. What happened is that
the Pharisees and other groups came together in Yavneh, a town
near the Mediterranean coast, and there they developed over a
period of years the main ideas of what we now know as
Rabbinic Judaism. "Yavneh" therefore serves as a kind of
symbol for response to crisis brought on by failed Messianism, a
symbol of rebuilding.

There is another symbol, also a place-name, "Massada."
Massada was a fortress near the Dead Sea, to which the surviving
Zealots and Messianists retreated for a last stand. As the end
drew near, with the Roman fortifications pressing upward on
the Jewish castle, the Zealots of Massada committed suicide.
Massada stands for bravery, for courage, and for fortitude. But
the end of zealous military courage was nihilistic, not much
different from the message of the apocalyptics. Yavneh stands
for something else. The people who came to Yavneh did not
fight, to be sure; they made their peace with the reality of
submission to Rome. If they were brave, it was not the courage
of the battlefield. But importantly, Yavneh did not end in

suicide but in the renaissance, the utter revolution in the history of Judaism, accomplished by Rabbinic Judaism. What is the great gesture of Yavneh, to match the grand, symbolic suicide of Massada?

A story about a leading rabbi, Yohanan ben Zakkai, and his disciple, Joshua ben Hananiah, tells us in a few words the grand gesture of Yavneh, the main outline of the Pharisaic-rabbinic view of the destruction:

> Once, as Rabbi Yohanan ben Zakkai was coming forth from Jerusalem, Rabbi Joshua followed after him and beheld the Temple in ruins.
> "Woe unto us," Rabbi Joshua cried, "that this, the place where the iniquities of Israel were atoned for, is laid waste!"
> "My son," Rabban Yohanan said to him, "be not grieved. We have another atonement as effective as this. And what is it? It is acts of loving-kindness, as it is said, *For I desire mercy and not sacrifice.*" [Hos. 6:6] (Avot de Rabbi Natan, Chap. 6)

How shall we relate the arcane rules about ritual purity to the public calamity faced by the heirs of the Pharisees at Yavneh? What connection exists between the ritual purity of the "kingdom of priests" and the atonement of sins in the Temple?

To Yohanan ben Zakkai, preserving the Temple was not an end in itself. He taught that there was another means of reconciliation between God and Israel, so that the Temple and its cult were not decisive. What really counted in the life of the Jewish people? Torah and piety. (We should add, Torah as taught by the Pharisees and, later on, by the rabbis, their continuators.) For the Zealots and Messianists of the day, the answer was power, politics, and the right to live under one's own rulers.

What was the will of God? It was doing deeds of loving-kindness: "I desire mercy, not sacrifice" (Hos. 6:6) meant to Yohanan, "We have a means of atonement as effective as the Temple, and it is doing deeds of loving-kindness." Just as willingly as people would contribute bricks and mortar for the rebuilding of a sanctuary, so they ought to contribute renunciation, self-sacrifice, and love, for the building of a sacred community. Earlier, Pharisaism had held that the Temple should be everywhere, especially in the home. Now Yohanan taught that sacrifice greater than the Temple's must characterize the life of the community. If one were to make an offering to God in a time when the Temple was no more, it must be the gift of selfless compassion. The holy altar must be the streets and marketplaces of the world, as, formerly, the purity of the Temple had to be observed in the streets and marketplaces of Jerusalem. In a sense, therefore, by making the laws of ritual purity incumbent upon the ordinary Jew, the Pharisees already had effectively limited the importance of the Temple and its cult. The earlier history of the Pharisaic sect thus had laid the groundwork for Yohanan ben Zakkai's response to Joshua ben Hananiah. It was a natural conclusion for one nurtured in a movement based upon the priesthood of all Israel.

Why did Yohanan ben Zakkai come to such an interpretation of the meaning of the life of Israel, the Jewish people? Because he was a Pharisee, and the Pharisaic party had long ago reached that same conclusion.

The Pharisees determined to concentrate on what they believed was really important in politics, and that was the fulfillment of all the laws of the Torah, even ritual tithing, and the elevation of the life of the people, even at home and in the streets, to what the Torah had commanded: You shall be a kingdom of priests and a holy people. A kingdom was envisioned in which everyone was a priest, a people all of whom were holy — a community which would live as if it were always in the Temple sanctuary of Jerusalem. Therefore, the purity laws, so complicated and inconvenient, were extended to the life of every Jew in the home. The Temple altar in Jerusalem would be replicated at the table of all Israel. To be sure, only a small minority of the Jewish people, to begin with, obeyed the law as taught by the Pharisaic party. Therefore, the group had to reconsider the importance of political life, through which the law might everywhere be effected. The party which had abandoned politics for piety now had to recover access to the instruments of power for the sake of piety. It was the way toward realization of what was essentially not a political aspiration.

THE OUTCOME

Of the four responses briefly outlined here, only the ones associated with the Christians and the Pharisees produced important historical consequences. The visionaries who lamented the past and hoped for near redemption enjoyed considerable success in sharing their vision with other Jews. The result was the Bar Kokhba War, 132-135 C.E., a disastrous repetition of the war which ended in 70. But no redemption followed; rather, severe repression for a time. Then the Pharisees' continuators, the rabbis led by a patriarch, gained complete control within the Jewish community of Palestine, and their program of attempting to make all Jews into priests, which to them meant into rabbis, was gradually effected.

The Qumran community did not survive the war, but its viewpoint seems to have persisted within the complex of Christian churches. For Christians, the events of August, 70, were not difficult to explain. Jesus had earlier predicted that the Temple would be destroyed; the Jews' own words had convicted them, as Matthew, writing in the aftermath of 70, claims, "Our blood be upon us and upon our children." But the new Temple and the new cult would go forward. The picture is complex, involving Jesus, become Christ, or the Church, embodying the new Temple, but the outcome is clear. The events of 70 served to confirm the new faith, and the faith itself supplied a new set of images to take over and exploit the symbols of the old cult.

The destruction of the Temple, Jerusalem, and the cult therefore marked a considerable transformation in the antecedent symbolic structures of Judaism. The ancient symbols were emptied of their old meanings and filled with new ones; they continued formally unchanged but substantively were in no way the same.

Faith of Torah: The Symbol of Torah

Let us now turn to the definition of the faith of Torah — Rabbinic Judaism. To do so, we review some of the ideas already presented and restate them in a systematic way.

A SCROLL OF TORAH

Central to Rabbinic Judaism is the belief that the ancient Scriptures constituted divine revelation, but only a part of it. At Sinai, God had handed down a dual revelation: the written part widely known, and the oral part preserved by the great scriptural heroes, passed on by prophets in the obscure past, finally and most openly handed down to the rabbis who created the Palestinian and Babylonian Talmuds. The "whole Torah" thus consisted of both written and oral parts. The rabbis taught that "whole Torah" was studied by David, augmented by Ezekiel, legislated by Ezra, and embodied in the schools and by the sages of every period in Israelite history from Moses to the present. It is a singular, linear conception of a revelation, preserved only by the few, pertaining to the many, and in time capable of bringing salvation to all.

The rabbinic conception of Torah further regards Moses as "our rabbi," the first and prototypical figure of the ideal Jew. It holds that whoever embodies the teachings of Moses "our rabbi" thereby conforms to the will of God — and not to God's will alone, but also to his *way*. In heaven, Rabbinic Judaism teaches, God and the angels study Torah just as rabbis do on earth. God dons phylacteries like a Rabbinic Jew. He prays in the rabbinic mode. He carries out the acts of compassion called for by Judaic ethics. He guides the affairs of the world according to the rules of Torah, just as does the rabbi in his court. One exegesis of the creation legend, as we saw, taught that God had looked into the Torah and therefrom had created the world.

The symbol of Torah is multidimensional. It includes the striking detail that whatever the most recent rabbi is destined to discover through proper exegesis of the tradition is as much a part of the Torah revealed to Moses as is a sentence of Scripture itself. It is therefore possible to participate even in the giving of the law by appropriate, logical inquiry into the law. God himself, studying and living by Torah, is believed to subject himself to these same rules of logical inquiry. If an earthly court overrules the testimony, delivered through miracles, of the heavenly one, God would rejoice, crying out, "My sons have conquered me!"

In a word, before us is a mythicoreligious system in which earth and heaven correspond to one another, with Torah — in place of Temple — model of both. The heavenly paradigm is embodied upon earth. Moses "our rabbi" is the pattern for the ordinary sage of the streets of Jerusalem, Pumbedita, Mainz, London, Lvov, Bombay, Dallas, or New York. And God himself participates in the system, for it is his image which, in the end, forms that cosmic paradigm. The faithful Jew constitutes the projection of the divine on earth. Honor is due to the learned rabbi more than to the scroll of the Torah, for through his learning and logic he may alter the very content of Mosaic revelation. He *is* Torah, not merely because he lives by it, but because at his best he forms as compelling an embodiment of the heavenly model as does a Torah scroll itself.

The final element in the rabbinic conception of Torah concerns salvation. It takes many forms. One salvific teaching holds that had Israel not sinned — that is, disobeyed the Torah — the Scriptures would have closed with the story of the conquest of Palestine. From that eschatological time forward, the sacred community would have lived in eternal peace under the divine law. Keeping the Torah was therefore the veritable guarantee of salvation. The opposite is said in many forms as well. Israel had sinned, therefore God had called the Babylonians and Romans to destroy the Temple of Jerusalem. But in his mercy he would restore the fortunes of the people when they, through their suffering and repentance, had expiated the result and the cause of their sin.

So in both negative and positive forms, the rabbinic idea of Torah tells of a necessary connection between the salvation of the people and of the world and the state of Torah among them. For example, if all Israel would properly keep a single Sabbath, the Messiah would come. Of special interest here is the rabbinic saying that the rule of the pagans depends upon the sin of Israel. If Israel would constitute a full and complete replication of "Torah," that is, of heaven, then pagan rule would come to an end. It would end because all Israel then, like some few rabbis even now, would attain to the creative powers inherent in Torah. Just as God had created the world through Torah, so saintly rabbis could create a sacred community. When Israel makes itself worthy through its embodiment of Torah, that is, through its perfect replication of heaven, then the end will come.

Learning thus finds a central place in the rabbinic tradition because of the belief that God had revealed his will to humankind through the medium of a written revelation, given to Moses at Mount Sinai, accompanied by oral traditions taught in the rabbinical schools and preserved in the Talmuds and related literature. The text without the oral traditions might have led elsewhere than into the academy, for the biblicism of other groups yielded something quite different from Jewish religious intellectualism, on which we shall dwell in the next chapter. But belief in the text was coupled with the belief that oral traditions were also revealed. In the books composed in the rabbinical academies, as much as in the Hebrew Bible itself, was contained God's will for humanity.

The act of study, memorization, and commentary upon the sacred books is holy. The study of sacred texts therefore assumes a *central* position in Judaism. Other traditions had their religious virtuosi whose virtuosity consisted in knowledge of a literary tradition; but few held, as does Judaism, that everyone must become such a virtuoso.

Traditional processes of learning are discrete and exegetical. Creativity is expressed not through abstract dissertation, but rather through commentary upon the sacred writings, or, more often in later times, commentary upon earlier commentaries. One might also prepare a code of the law, but such a code represented little more than an assemblage of authoritative opinions of earlier times, with a decision being offered upon those few questions the centuries had left unanswered.

The chief glory of the commentators is their *hiddush*, "novelty." The *hiddush* constitutes a scholastic disquisition upon a supposed contradiction between two earlier authorities, chosen from any period, with no concern for how they might in fact relate historically, and upon a supposed harmonization of their "contradiction." Or a new distinction might be read into an ancient law, upon which basis ever more questions might be raised and solved. The focus of interest quite naturally lies upon law, rather than theology, history, philosophy, or other sacred sciences. Within the law it rests upon legal theory, and interest in the practical consequences of the law is decidely subordinated.

The devotion of the Jews to study of the Torah, as here defined, is held by them to be their chief glory. This sentiment is repeated in song and prayer, and shapes the values of the common society. The important Jew is learned. The child many times is blessed, starting at birth, "May he grow in Torah, commandments, good deeds."

The central *ritual* of the rabbinic tradition, therefore, is study. Study as a natural action entails learning traditions and executing them — in this context, in school or in court. Study becomes a *ritual action* when it is endowed with values *extrinsic* to its ordinary character, when set into a mythic context. When disciples memorize their masters' traditions and actions, they participate in the rabbinic view of Torah as the organizing principle of reality. Their study is thereby endowed with the sanctity that ordinarily pertains to prayer or other cultic matters. Study loses its referent in intellectual attainment. The *act* of study itself becomes holy, so that its original purpose, which was mastery of particular information, ceases to matter much. What matters is piety, piety expressed through the rites of studying. Repeating the words of the oral revelation, even without comprehending them, might produce reward, just as imitating the masters matters, even without really being able to

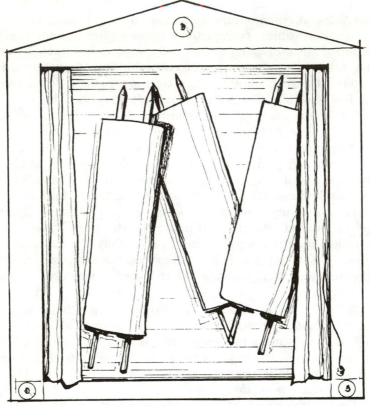

AN ARK FOR TORAH SCROLLS

explain the reasons for their actions. The separation of the value, or sanctity, of the act of study from the natural, cognitive result of learning therefore transforms studying from a natural to a ritual action. That separation is accomplished in part by the rabbis' conception of Torah, and in part by the powerful impact of the academic environment itself.

A striking illustration of the distinction between mere learning and learning as part of ritual life derives from the comment of Mar Zutra, a fifth-century C.E. Babylonian rabbi, on Isaiah 14:5: "The Lord has broken the staff of the wicked, the scepter of rulers." The rabbi said, "These are disciples of the sages who teach public laws to boorish judges." The fact that the uncultivated judge would know the law did not matter, for he still was what he had been, a boor, not a disciple of the sages.

Mere knowledge of the laws does not transform an ordinary person, however powerful, into a sage. Learning carried with it more than naturalistic valence, as further seen in the saying of Amemar, a contemporary of Mar Zutra: "A sage is superior to a prophet, as Scripture says, 'And a prophet has a heart of wisdom' " (Ps. 90:12). What characterized the prophet was, Amemar said, sagacity. Since the prophet was supposed to reveal the divine will, it was not inconsequential that his revelation depended *not* upon gifts of the spirit but upon *learning*.

The rabbi functioned in the Jewish community as judge and administrator. But he lived in a society in some ways quite separate from that of Jewry as a whole. The rabbinical academy was, first, a law school. Some of its graduates served as judges and administrators of the law. The rabbinical school was by no means a center for merely legal study. It was, like the Christian monastery, the locus for a peculiar kind of religious living. Only one of its functions concerned those parts of the Torah to be applied in everyday life through the judiciary.

The school, or *Yeshiva* (literally, "session"), was a council of Judaism, a holy community. In it men learned to live holy lives and to become saints, that is, holy masters of Torah. When they left, sages continued to live by the discipline of the school. They invested great efforts in teaching that discipline, by example and precept, to ordinary folk. Through the school Rabbinic Judaism transformed the Jewish people into its vision of the true replica of Mosaic revelation.

The schools, like other holy communities, imposed their own particular rituals, intended, in the first instance, for the disciples and masters. Later, it was hoped, all Jews would conform to those rituals and so join the circle of master and disciples.

As with study, the schools' discipline transformed other ordinary, natural actions, gestures, and functions into rituals — the rituals of "being a rabbi." Everyone ate; rabbis did so in a "rabbinic" manner. That is to say, what others regarded as matters of mere etiquette, formalities and conventions intended to render eating aesthetically agreeable, rabbis regarded as matters of "Torah," something to be *learned*. It was "Torah" to do things one way, and it was equally "ignorance" to do them another (though not heresy, for theology was no issue).

The master of Torah, whether disciple or teacher, would

demonstrate his mastery not merely through the discussion of legal traditions or his actions in court; he would do so by how he sat at the table, by what ritual formulas he recited before eating one or another kind of fruit or vegetable, by how he washed his hands. Everyone had to relieve himself. The sage would do so according to "Torah." The personality traits of individuals might vary. Those expected of, and inculcated into, a sage were of a single fabric.

We must keep in mind the fundamental difference between the way of Torah and ways to salvation explored by other holy people and sacred communities. The rabbi at no point would admit that his particular rites were imposed upon him alone, apart from all Israel. He ardently "spread Torah" among the Jews at large. He believed he had to, because Torah was revealed to all Israel at Sinai and required of all Israel afterward. If he was right that Moses was "our rabbi" and even God kept the commandments, then he had to ask of everyone what he demanded of himself: conformity to the *halakhah*, the way of Torah. His task was facilitated by the widespread belief that Moses had indeed revealed the Torah and that some sort of interpretation quite naturally was required to apply it to everyday affairs. The written part of Torah generally shaped the life of ordinary pious folk. What the rabbi had to accomplish was to persuade them that the written part of the Torah was partial and incomplete, requiring further elaboration through the oral traditions he alone possessed and embodied.

The Aftermath of Disaster

When the Temple was destroyed, it is clear, the foundations of the country's religious-cultural life were destroyed. The Temple had constituted one of the primary, unifying elements in that common life. The structure not only of political life and of society, but also of the imaginative life of the country, depended upon the Temple and its worship and cult. It was there that people believed they served God. At the Temple the lines of structure — both cosmic and social — converged. The Temple, moreover, served as the basis for those many elements of autonomous self-government and political life left in the Jews' hands by the Romans. Consequently, the destruction of the Temple meant not merely a significant alteration in the cultic or ritual life of the Jewish people, but also a profound and far-reaching crisis in their inner and spiritual existence.

A viable cultural-religious existence was reconstructed during the next half-century, for between ca. 70 and ca. 120, we know in retrospect, a number of elements of the religious-cultural structure of the period before 70 were put together into a new synthesis, the synthesis we now call Rabbinic Judaism. In response to the disaster of the destruction Rabbinic Judaism took shape, and its success was in its capacity to claim things had not changed at all — hence the assertion that even at the start, Moses was "our rabbi" — while making the very destruction of the Temple itself into the verification and vindication of the new structure. Rabbinic Judaism claimed that it was possible to serve God not only through sacrifice, but also through study of Torah. A priest is in charge of the life of the community, but a new priest, the rabbi. The old sin-offerings still may be carried out through deeds of loving-kindness; indeed, when the whole Jewish people will fully carry out the teachings of the Torah, the Temple itself will be rebuilt. To be sure, the Temple will be reconstructed along lines laid out in the Torah — that is, in the whole Torah of Moses, the Torah taught by the rabbis. Like the prophets and historians in the time of the first destruction, in 586 B.C.E., the rabbis further claimed that it was because the people had sinned, had not kept the Torah, that the Temple had been destroyed. So the disaster itself was made to vindicate the rabbinic teaching and to verify its truth.

Now let us stand back from this synthesis and ask, How was it put together? What are its primary elements? What trends or movements before 70 are represented by these elements?

Two primary components in the Yavneh synthesis before 70 are to be discerned: first, the emphases of Pharisaism, and second, the values of the scribal profession. Pharisaism lay stress upon universal keeping of the law, obligating every Jew to do what only the elite — the priests — were normally expected to accomplish. The professional ideal of the scribes stressed the study of Torah and the centrality of the learned person in the religious system.

The unpredictable, final element in the synthesis of Pharisaic stress on widespread law, including ritual-law, observance and scribal emphasis on learning, is what makes Rabbinic Judaism distinctive, and that is the conviction that the community now stands in the place of the Temple. The ruins of the cult, after all, did not mark the end of the collective life of Israel. What survived was the *people*. It was the genius of Rabbinic Judaism to recognize that the people might reconstitute the Temple in its own collective life. Therefore the people had to be made holy, as the Temple had been holy, and the people's social life had to be sanctified as the surrogate for what had been lost. The rabbinic ideal further maintained that the rabbi served as the new priest, the study of Torah substituted for the Temple sacrifice, and deeds of loving-kindness were the social surrogate for the sin-offering — personal sacrifice instead of animal sacrifice.

We have now considered the way in which Rabbinic Judaism took shape. We know the meaning of its central symbol, Torah, and we have some idea of the institutions created to express it, and the emphasis of life within it. We understand that it was through learning in the broadest sense that the rabbis would carry out their concept of Torah. It is now time to ask, What is the nature of rabbinic learning? What are the processes of Torah? And, of still greater interest, what is the substance, the result, of learning in Torah? Since the rabbinic way of life produced a pattern of everyday behavior, including prayer as well as study, we shall ask about the way in which the Rabbinic Jews interpreted everyday life. How was and is the individual understood? What was and is the conception of the family? How did and does Rabbinic Judaism view the life of the Jewish people? What is the rabbinic idea of God and of the world? In other words, we have completed our survey of the formation of Rabbinic Judaism. Now we want to know about its contents.

Notes

1.   Mishnah Avot 1:1.
2.   Quoted from Louis Ginzberg, *The Legends of the Jews*, trans. Henrietta Szold (Philadelphia: Jewish Publication Society, 1947), Vol. I, p. 3. Rev. ed. 1961.

3. Midrash Rabbah to Genesis 1:1. Quoted from *Midrash Rabbah*, ed. H. Freedman and M. Simon (London: The Soncino Press, 1939), Vol. I, p. 1.
4. Babylonian Talmud Berakhot 55a.

Chapter Two
The Structure of Judaism:
Torah, God, Israel

The Process of Torah: Midrash

How shall we describe the timeless, enduring mode of being that was laid forth by the rabbis of the early centuries of the Common Era? The way of Torah is contained and expressed in certain books. These books begin with the written Scriptures. We seriously misunderstand the concept of Torah if we suppose that the written Scriptures tell the whole story. But we also err if we ignore the centrality of the written Scriptures, Tanakh, in the unfolding of Rabbinic Judaism. On the contrary, Tanakh is the prime source of Rabbinic Judaism, of Torah. The reading of the Tanakh in synagogue worship — a passage from Pentateuch, the five books of Moses, and a passage from the prophetic writings — is the central act of prayer. The prayers themselves consist in large part of quotations of biblical literature. The writings of the prophets, Psalms, Proverbs: these are the formative elements of Judaic piety. Yet, as we now know, Tanakh is read through the eye of the rabbis, understood as they understand it, and applied in the light of their interpretation.

The key to the process by which Torah came into being is contained in this last word, interpretation. Through the careful, disciplined reading of the Holy Scriptures, the Tanakh, the

47

rabbis located eternal truths. They had a name for the process, *midrash*, derived from the root *darash*, to seek, investigate. Let us now consider the process of the "creation" of Torah, the discovery of revelation and participation in the process of revelation.

Holy Scripture posed to the rabbis a more perplexing problem than simply uncovering the plain meaning of the sacred words. Their problem, which still troubles book- or text-centered religions, was how to discover in ancient writings continuing truths and meaning for a very different time. Their answer to this problem, as we just saw, is in *Midrash*, the exegesis and exposition of revealed Scripture. In truth, Scriptural interpretation is as old as Scripture, and elements of *Midrash* are presented in the Hebrew Bible itself. The particular achievement of the sages was to explore the implications of *Midrash* and to exploit its formidable techniques in the case of a sophisticated and highly contemporary religion.

The rabbis found that they had to expound the religion of a text ascribed to Moses, who had preceded them by much more than a millennium, in the first centuries of the Common Era. They had to make sense out of the great teachings of the past, and to apply them to the present situation. Far more than this, they had to come to grips with the details of the Scripture that conveyed these truths. The sages were concerned not only with the content, but with the very context of revelation. Their inheritance was a record of revelation whose minutest detail demanded assent from the pious Jew. If these ancient words were to bear truth for all time, they had to make good sense always and everywhere. The rabbis would not, therefore, pass silently over some bothersome detail which did not harmonize with their idea of truth or good manners. They would not deny the Bible's claim to detailed authenticity. "If it is empty — from you," that is, if you see no meaning in a verse, the fault is yours. Scripture could not be reduced to an essence; every word was somehow essential.

Confronted with some biblical incident that did not accord with accepted morality, the rabbis could not dismiss the matter as inconsequential. At the same time, they could not justify an ethical outrage by pointing out the primitive standards of an ancient generation. If, like modern critics, they were to explain some improper action as evidence of the antiquity of a given passage, they would thereby have confessed that Scripture bore relevance to the archaeologist or historian of religion, but by no means offered appropriate instruction for a more advanced age. The rabbis would not claim that the more detailed precepts of Scriptures were addressed to one particular generation (except where the Bible itself makes this clear). They would not admit that its truth was relative, appropriate only to an early, savage time. To them the truth of the Bible was eternal, standing as an imperative to humankind.

This problem continues to perplex people. The Bible speaks to a primitive and naive universe. Has the passage of time muted its voice? Liberals in days past used to say that the Bible is not a textbook for natural science. But liberals did not believe in revelation. Fundamentalists offered ingenious explanations for the real intent of Scripture; for example, the seven days of Creation represent seven aeons of time. But the Bible does not say so. Must a person share the Biblical viewpoint on theology, cosmology, and anthropology in order to hold on to its ultimate consequence of faith in God and in the message of religion? History forced upon the sages a search for harmony between the detailed text and the contemporary view of metaphysics. This search was not the consequence of negation, but of affirmation.

In the *Midrash*, the rabbis were not intentionally traditional. They did not wonder how to save a text they might already have come to doubt, nor did they set out to sustain Scripture as a possibility for their piety. For the sages Torah had made manifest the emergent truth that underlies all things. It was the divine design for the universe. To contrive to demonstrate harmony between current truth and Torah would be to reveal the obvious. Revelation was eternal and always in harmony with new visions of the truth. If the rabbis were traditionalists, they never knew it.

The Bible itself made Midrashic elucidation possible. The very first word of God was light. Commenting on Jeremiah 23:29, the Talmud says, " 'Is not my word like fire,' saith the Lord, 'and like a hammer which breaks the rock into pieces?' (Jer. 23:29): Just as a hammer strikes the anvil and kindles clouds of sparks, so does Scripture yield many meanings, as it is said, 'Once did God speak, but two things have I heard . . .' (Ps. 62:11)." The rabbis assumed that Torah is the indivisible, exhaustive account of the event of revelation at Sinai. It reveals some truth and encompasses all truth. Hence it was their task to draw out of the given text the widest possible range of religious insight. They did not need to distinguish between the obvious sense of words and subtler secondary meanings. Plain sense (*peshat*) is simply what was immediately apparent. *Midrash* was the level of meaning discovered by search (*derash*), by disciplined and careful exegesis. The truth was one, but the rabbis came upon the part uncovered by *Midrash* with a little more effort. (It is true that the rabbis did distinguish occasionally between a particularly imaginative *Midrash* of a verse and its plain sense, but this distinction meant far less to them than it does today.)

A classic exposition of the nature of *Midrash* is in Professor Shalom Spiegel's introduction to *Legends of the Jews* by Louis Ginzberg, in which he writes:

> Just as a pearl results from a stimulus in the shell of a mollusk, so also a legend may arise from an irritant in Scripture. The legend of Cain and Lamech has its foothold in two passages of Scripture. One passage tells of a sign granted by Cain as a warning to all who might threaten his life: Anyone that slays Cain shall suffer seven-fold vengeance. (Gen. 4:15) The other is the address of Lamech to his wives, reckless with swagger or savagery: I kill a man for just wounding me! (Gen. 4:25)
>
> This is a brutal and bad boast in a book such as the Bible, but in reality it is less bothersome than the earlier statement in Genesis 4:15 . . . . After all, the bluster of a braggart or bully need not be believed literally . . . . Genesis 4:15 cannot be so lightly dismissed . . . . The pledge given to Cain presupposes a peculiarly ferocious form of blood-feud: Any attack on the bearer of the sign is to be avenged by the slaughter of seven members of the tribe to which the assailant belonged. The archaeologist might conclude . . . that some of the stories in the book of Genesis preserve exceedingly ancient traditions . . . often antedating by centuries the birth of Biblical religion . . . . But in all times men have turned to the Bible not only for antiquarian curiosities, but for spiritual uplift and guidance. To such readers it

must be distressing . . . to find the Holy Writ ascribing to the Deity itself the acceptance without protest of an institution of primitive law . . . . Many will prefer to believe that this cannot be the meaning of the sacred writings . . . .

When facts or texts become unacceptable, fiction or legend weaves the garland of nobler fancy. This is how the story of Cain's slaying was born . . .

The tale runs: Lamech was a burly but blind giant who loved to follow the chase under the guidance of his son, Tubal-Cain. Whenever the horn of a beast came in sight, the boy would tell his father to shoot at it with a bow and arrow. One day he saw a horn move between two hills; he turned Lamech's arrow upon it. The aim was good, the quarry dropped to the ground. When they came close to the victim, the lad exclaimed: "Father, thou hast killed something that resembles a human being in all respects, except it carries a horn on its forehead!" Lamech knew at once what had happened: he had killed his ancestor Cain, who had been marked by God with a horn for his own protection, "lest anyone who came upon him should kill him." (Gen. 4:15) In bitter remorse Lamech wept: "I killed a man to my wounding!" (Gen. 4:24)

What seemed to be shocking Scripture was made by this legend to yield a moral tale. Genesis 4:24 was turned from a barbarian boast into a cry of contrition: The offensive "I kill a man for just wounding me" was now read "I killed a man to *my* wounding and sorrow." The Hebrew permits this change by a mere inflection of voice. But above all, the stumbling block in Genesis 4:15 was removed: the assurance of the deity that Cain's vengeance shall be sevenfold was made to mean that his punishment will be exacted from him in the seventh generation. His sentence was to be carried out by Lamech, the seventh in the succession of generations since Adam. The savage reprisal . . . became a deserved but deferred penalty, the merciful Judge, slow to anger, granting the sinner a long reprieve to repent and mend his ways. In brief, two passages of the sacred Writ, disturbing the peace and disquieting the faith of a host of pious readers in every age, were metamorphosed in this legend of Cain and Lamech to yield the edifying lesson: even the arrow of a sightless archer obeys the holy will and word of God.

. . . Any vestige of reprehensible or primitive practices was read away, and Scripture brought to conform to the advanced conscience of a later state in civilization.

A second type of *Midrash* was inquiry into the legal portions of the Pentateuch to discover laws to apply to a new situation, or to uncover Scriptural basis for an apparent innovation in law. An example of such legal *Midrash* was the effort to demonstrate the real meaning of "an eye for an eye." The sages held that the verse clearly means that one should exact the monetary equivalent of an eye for the loss of an eye, and no more. One proof, among many brought by the Talmud, is derived from Numbers 35:31, "Thou shalt not take ransom for the life of a murderer . . ." This means, "for the life of a murderer thou shalt not take ransom, but thou shalt take ransom for limbs." Scripture thus means, and has always meant, that a ransom may compensate loss of a major limb. We shall return to this matter.

Midrash represents, therefore, creative philology and creative historiography. As creative philology, the *Midrash* discovers meaning in apparently meaningless detail. It creates out of the fabric of silence as of speech. As Dr. Max Kadushin demonstrates in *The Rabbinic Mind*, the *Midrash* uses the elements of language not as fixed, unchanging categories, but as relative, living, tentative nuances of thought. As creative historiography, the *Midrash* rewrites the past to make manifest the eternal rightness of Scriptural paradigms. What would it be like if all people lived at one moment? This the *Midrash* sets out to reveal, justifying David by the criteria of Stoic philosophy and even by Roman law, and thundering pious curses at the heads of people behaving in accord with the morality of their own age. *Midrash* thus exchanges stability of language and the continuity of history for stability of values and the eternity of truth.

In the Bible, the rabbis treasured a many-splendored jewel, now to be admired in one light, now in another. Each word has many modulations of meaning, awaiting the sensitive touch of a troubled soul to unfold a special message for a particular moment in time. *Midrash* teaches that for all times and to all times and to all people, Scriptural values are congruous and consistent. Lamech and a man living fifteen centuries later are judged by the same ethics, for Scripture and its people are wholly in harmony with the sophisticated morality of any age. History does not apply to revelation. There are no relative truths. Revelation happened under the aspect of eternity: one God, one Torah, one truth for all humankind in every age.

The Essentials of Rabbinic Literature:
Mishnah and Talmud

The Mishnah is the first and most important document of Rabbinic Judaism. It reached its present form at about the beginning of the third century C.E. and is based upon traditions at least two hundred years older than that; some fundamental concepts and traditions themselves may go back, in content but not in exact language, to the first century before the Common Era.

The Mishnah is essentially a law code. It is divided into six major parts, called *Seders* or Orders, encompassing the vast themes of "reality" covered by the Oral Torah. These are, first, agricultural law; second, Sabbath and festival laws; third, family laws; fourth, civil and criminal laws; fifth, laws concerning sacrifices in the cult; and, finally, laws concerning purities.

To use more general language, Mishnah deals with the Torah's governance of the economy and means of production, the material basis of life (agriculture); the organization and differentiation of time into the holy and the profane (Sabbath and festivals); the structure and definition of the family, in particular the rights of women; the regulation of society and human interactions and transactions outside of the family; the mode of service to the divinity through sacrifice and cult; and the regulation of the unseen world of purity and impurity as these affect the cult, society, the economy, and the home. The "theory" of the Mishnah, therefore, is that all of reality is to be suitably organized and rationally governed through the law of Mishnah.

Since the Mishnah is the fundamental document of Rabbinic Judaism, it is worth taking some time to understand it. For that purpose, we shall conduct a mental experiment. We shall try to see what we should produce if we were to attempt to create our own Mishnah, by asking what areas of everyday life we should include, and how these several aspects of life fit together into a larger picture of reality.

If you had to put down on paper, in a few words, everything you believe important about anything, what form would your thoughts take? How would you convey, in a few simple words, your conception of reality, your idea of how things are and should be? That is the work of the creative men and women in each generation, in every civilization: to grasp and express the whole, a vision of the largest things, in a simple way. Obviously, it is through religion that men and women have attempted to express their vast conception of being, of all reality. Yet you realize that religions differ; they not only express different thoughts, but they do so in different modes of speaking. The characteristic way in which Rabbinic Judaism speaks its great ideas is through what we call "laws." By "law," you probably understand such things as not stealing, or "no parking," or not lying under oath. But to Rabbinic Judaism, law is meant to express, to encompass, all of reality. Law is too small a word to make room for all which, in Rabbinic Judaism, we know as *halakhah*, the way things are and should be.

Precisely what are the topics important to the rabbis of the Mishnah and the Talmud? Into what components do they divide this "reality" of which we have spoken? Let us consider the major divisions of Mishnah and, translated into our own terms, their topics and subject matter.

First, comes the section on "Seeds," that is, on agricultural laws. Why first? What laws? Farming comes first because the Jews made their living by farming. "If there is no bread, there is no Torah." We start with the most practical concern anyone has: to make a living. But what is it about farming that interested the rabbis? What are the "laws"? Their primary topic encompasses the ways in which farmers should do their work in accord with Torah. The Torah contains many "laws" about farming, and the purpose of most of these laws is to teach people how to express their thanks to God for what God gives.

The way thought appropriate, both in the Written Torah and in the Oral Torah which is Mishnah, is to give for sacred purposes a part of the yield of the field and the farm, to observe those rites and restrictions revealed in the Torah about how farming was to be carried on—planting which seeds with which, giving what proportion of the crop to the poor (for helping the poor is serving God), giving what proportion to the priest, the teacher of Torah, keeping what sort of seed separate from what other sort of seed, and so on.

If you were an anthropologist visiting a strange tribe in the South Seas and there you noticed that people "religiously" avoided planting, let us say, grape vines and corn or wheat together, you would call that a "taboo." The Mishnah, like the Written Torah, begins with farming "taboos." And these, it is clear, concern farming. If you were a theologian who had as your task to state, in clear and modern language, the meaning of faith, you would phrase matters thus: God is served through the course of nature upon which our lives depend. And what is that mode of service?

Here you need only open Scriptures to find the theologian's answer. "You shall be holy because I am holy," Scripture says, and then it spells matters out, in part, in terms of agricultural "taboos." Why? Because when God made the world, He made things in a certain way, in accord with a certain sense of order. Things should be whole, complete, fit naturally together. That is what creation is all about, the formation of order out of chaos. In the life of the farm, what in particular are the modes of orderly life? That question is answered in very specific ways, by the "laws" about giving the priest his various offerings, or keeping seeds separate, or donating a share of the crop to the poor, and so forth. Let us return to our theologian. What does he call this? He opens Scriptures and finds, "You shall be *holy*." Holiness is expressed in these laws, holiness meaning order, wholeness, completeness. So the first work of holiness is the sanctification of economic life, making our living in a way which expresses God's will.

Again, why start with farming, with ways in which we express our sense of holiness through agriculture? Because the rabbis are practical people, and they know that life depends upon food, clothing, shelter; life begins with the necessities of life, and these—in that setting—are provided through our work on the soil.

If you wanted to write a Mishnah for the United States or Canada, you would begin with laws about factories, farms, schools, government, the conduct of a lawyer's or a doctor's office, of a store—the ways in which our society today makes its living. You would want to convey a sense of the wholeness, completeness, order, and form of our economy. You would want to show the ways in which our work is, or can and should be, holy, whole.

These ways, it should be clear, will include many matters we commonly regard as ethical: teachings about how one person should treat another. But you will not understand Judaism in its classical form if you think that all things come down to the practical question of relations between one person and the next. Ethics is a part of a much larger conception of reality. Ethics, just as much as ritual or "taboo," expresses that conception. But your Mishnah of the factory or the store will tell the worker or the storekeeper more than that he or she should be honest or considerate. That much is clear.

Let us go back to the Mishnah of the rabbis of ancient times. What is their second topic?

We work, but we also rest. And we know we should rest because of the passage of time. After our interest in the economic, the material basis of life, we turn to the rhythm of time, of work and of rest, energy and fatigue. So the second division of the Mishnah is called "Seasons" or—again to use the language of the anthropologists—"taboos" about holy days. On this day, one does so and so, on that day one does not—the rites and rituals of dividing time into "holy" and "profane." Naturally, the Sabbath comes first, for it is the Sabbath which is The Holy Day. This topic is divided into two sides or aspects: (1) the meaning of Sabbath holiness for labor and (2) the meaning of holiness of time for space. That last point is difficult. The Written Torah says that, on the Sabbath, we should stay home. [*"Let no man leave his place on the seventh day."* (Exodus 16:29)] The Mishnah, the Oral Torah, takes up this rule and asks, "How far away is still home?" What is the effect of the Sabbath upon the space we occupy? "Seasons" proceed to various holy days, Passover, Sukkot, the Day of Atonement, the New Year, and other topics anyone familiar with the Jewish calendar could predict.

So, from the *material* basis of society, we proceed to the *temporal* or time basis. We make a living. We do it on one day, but not on another. We have something like a set of horizontals and verticals. The horizontals are the ongoing, everyday things we do to make a living. The vertical lines divide the horizontals, as I said, distinguishing "making a living" in material, economic terms from "making a life." If we ask ourselves how we should write the Mishnah of "time" or "seasons" in America, we might call our tractates "Labor Day," "New Year's Eve," "What are you doing Saturday night?" and so on. The point is clear.

We eat. We live from day to day. And we do this in society, with other people, with families. So the natural third division concerns the family. And here the rabbis express a very simple conception of the family. They call the division of the Mishnah dealing with family affairs: "Women." Their idea is that women are the foundation of the home and family. Their deepest concern is to protect, define, and defend the rights of women. How does a family begin? It begins with a document which defines the rights and duties of women and of their husbands. How does a family end? It ends with a document which effects divorce, freeing the woman to build a new house and a new family, providing for her maintenance in the interval between the divorce and the (taken for granted) remarriage. If you wrote a Mishnah on women today, of course your specific tractates would be different for society is very different from what it was. Yet it is absolutely certain that, if you tried to put down on paper your conception of how "reality" is and should be, how "all of life" is organized, you would have to devote much of your thought to the meaning and role of being male and being female, to the way in which male and female become one, one flesh, one family. Perhaps your tractates would include "Adolescence" and "The Torah of Dating." But in the center of the life of society is the woman, her role, her duties, her tasks: to build society.

We eat. We live from day to day. We create families. And families live together in society. They bump up against one another. They hurt one another, damage one another's property, and come into conflict with one another. What is that deep sense of order, balance, wholeness which governs the conflicts between individuals? That is the natural next problem, and it is dealt with in the fourth division of the Mishnah, which is called—given the nature of the human heart and the quality of human relationships—"Damages." For when people come into contact they commonly come into conflict. And it is conflict, aggression, and property rights which have to be worked out in an orderly way.

Curiously, it is at this point that the rabbis of the Mishnah introduce how we transfer property from one person to another, how we adjudicate conflicting claims of all sorts. I suppose the reason is that they recognized, took account of, and meant even to sanctify that "base" but natural component of everyone's heart: owning things, property. And, since families are built upon homes and possessions which one generation means to assemble for the benefit of the next, it is natural that after we attend to the basic building block of society—the family and the woman who makes the home—we turn to the dynamic relationships within society: property, damages of persons and property, and the like.

This is the point at which what you understand by "law" and what Mishnah gives us as *halakhah* come together. If you were to go to law school, you would study a great deal about torts and damages, property and the transfer of property, the rights of individuals to own and to dispose of the fruit of their labor, not to mention the way courts are set up and how they do their business (in the Mishnah, *Tractate Sanhedrin*), oaths in court and oaths for other purposes, and the like.

There is nothing surprising here except for one fact: To Rabbinic Judaism, all of this is part of Torah, a matter of religion. Indeed, if you study in a yeshivah, it is likely that one of the first talmudic tractates you will learn will be selected from this fourth division of the Mishnah. And the reason is that holiness is not merely rite, ritual, or "taboo" — something in our minds and imagination — but, especially, holiness governs the conduct of everyday life, of *law* in the commonplace practical sense.

That fact is so obvious that we may proceed forthwith from the most obvious to the least obvious, from the first four divisions of the Mishnah to the last two, one on the "Sacrifices" and how they are to be offered, the other on "Purity" and impurity. The fifth division takes up those many biblical laws on how God is served through sacrifice. What the rabbis try to do is spell out the deeper meanings of those laws. Obviously, we could compose many tractates for our modern Mishnah on the service of God through rite. We should have a tractate on conduct in the synagogue or temple. We should want a tractate on prayer, on the organization of our service of worship. Those who construct "creative services" may want to figure out some logic, some order, for their work: On the Sabbath, one plays a guitar with five strings.

And then there is that mysterious division, the sixth division of the Mishnah, on purities. To understand the dynamics of these laws, we turn first to an analogy. There are things which we cannot see but which we know are present. Take, for instance, atomic radiation. If you were to go into an area contaminated by radiation, you might see nothing and feel nothing, but that does not mean you are not affected. You are contaminated; and if you do not wash or wear protective clothing against severe radiation, you will become very sick and may die. Further, things which you wear may be contaminated and they may, in turn, infect others with contamination.

Now, in the books of Leviticus and Numbers, the Written Torah tells about various sources and modes of contamination, of things which make a person unclean. In all ways, the result is the same: A person who is "unclean" cannot come into the holy place. These various sources of contamination have one thing in common: They break the order of nature, the wholeness and completeness of life. Death breaks the balance of life. The corpse is unclean. Various sorts of animals or insects are conceived — for reasons that do not concern us — as "unclean." If you touch them, you are unclean. Since it is in the sanctuary, the holy temple, that the wholeness or completeness of life is most fully realized, the person who has somehow broken with the natural balance and order of creation cannot go there. The rabbis of the Mishnah take up this conception and work it out in exquisite detail.

I suppose it would be hardest to write our modern version of that sixth division. Yet perhaps there are unseen realities, unfelt yet deeply perceived relationships, which can serve as an analogy in our own day for the strange and mysterious concepts of "cleanness" and "uncleanness" of the time of the Mishnah. I offered earlier a very significant analogy, contamination by unseen radiation. Yet, are there spiritual comparisons which we can draw? Is there something a person can do, for example, which so transforms him or her as to remove that person from the realm of the "normal"? And I do not mean some practical deed which is unethical or immoral. I mean, can we go to some *place* which is "unclean," which leaves us with a sense of filth and disorder, even because of our mere presence at or contact with that place? I tend to think that such a place is a place in which our mere presence leaves us with the sense of a need to wash ourselves and make ourselves clean. And there *are* such places, and uncleanness applies not only to place but also to persons, even to objects.

So, in a few brief words, that is the Mishnah — the Torah which contains, in its few brief words, the whole concept of reality constructed by the rabbis of ancient times and conceived by them to have been revealed by God at Mount Sinai to Moses, along with the Written Torah which we call *Tanakh* or the Hebrew Bible, and the Christians call the Old Testament.[1]

Let us now turn to a passage of Mishnah and consider its literary traits and legal substance. The passage concerns personal damages: What is the law if Peter breaks John's leg? The answer follows. We assess Peter with monetary damages, and we have to reckon how to translate the breaking of a leg into fair compensation.

The Mishnah paragraph is the first in the Eighth Chapter of *Bava Qamma*, The First Gate, laws on civil damages. It is given in the translation by E. W. Kirzner, published by The Soncino Press, London (pp. 473-474), as part of *The Babylonian Talmud*, a complete and reliable translation into English of that fundamental document of Judaism.

> Mishnah. One who injures a fellow man becomes liable to him for five items: (1) For depreciation, (2) for pain, (3) for healing, (4) for loss of time and (5) for degradation.
>
> How is it with (1) "depreciation"? If he put out his eye, cut off his arm or broke his leg, the injured person is considered as if he were a slave being sold in the market place, and a valuation is made as to how much he was worth [previously], and how much he is worth [now].
>
> (2) "Pain" — if he burnt him either with a spit or with a nail, even though on his [finger] nail which is a place where no bruise could be made, it has to be calculated how much a man of equal standing would require to be paid to undergo such pain.

(3) "Healing" — if he has struck him, he is under obligation to pay medical expenses. Should ulcers [meanwhile] arise on his body, if as a result of the wound, the offender would be liable, but if not as a result of the wound, he would be exempt. Where the wound was healed but reopened, healed again but reopened, he would still be under obligation to heal him. If, however, it had completely healed [but had subsequently reopened] he would no more be under obligation to heal him.

(4) "Loss of time" — the injured person is considered as if he were a watchman of cucumber beds [as even a lame or one-armed person could be employed in this capacity] [so that the loss of such wages (but not of the previous employment on account of the reason which follows) sustained by him during the period of illness may be reimbursed to him], for there has already been paid to him the value of his hand or the value of his leg [through which deprivation he would no more be able to carry on his previous employment].

(5) "Degradation" — all to be estimated in accordance with the status of the offender and the offended.

The passage of the Mishnah we have before us thus specifies the five sorts of damages one has to pay if he or she damages someone else. We ask how we assess "depreciation"; then we want to know how to translate "pain" into dollars and cents. Third comes healing, which of course means the payment of medical expenses. But we forthwith have to ask about expenses for secondary costs, that is, for healing an ailment not directly caused by the original act of damage. This is relatively easy to calculate, as is the fourth item, loss of time. Finally, we include a peculiarly human matter, embarrassment or degradation.

Before we proceed, let us make a few observations about the paragraph of Mishnah we have just read.

First, ask yourself this question: Does the Mishnah follow the literary style of Tanakh? The answer quite obviously is that it does not. While this may be "Oral Torah" or "the second Torah" in some important way, no effort has been made to copy the biblical modes of formulation and expression. The second Torah is stylistically independent and autonomous of the first.

Second, what is the presupposition of this law? It is that a person who injures someone must compensate him or her, and is not punished — as Scripture explicitly states — by having to suffer an equivalent punishment. The one thing Mishnah ignores is: *An eye for an eye, a tooth for a tooth.* (Exod. 21:24) What sort of Torah is this, which takes as its basic assumption the exact opposite of what the written Torah explicitly demands? We have already alluded to the problem in our discussion of the nature of midrash. Now we see the problem fully exposed.

Third, when we turn to the substance of the law, we find a careful effort to supply guidelines applicable everywhere. We do not specify compensation in terms likely to be relevant to one country or one brief period of time. We calculate in terms relative to all times. "How much a man of equal standing would require to be paid . . ." "Loss of Wages . . ." "The status of the offender and the offended" — these all are efforts to avoid such specificity as would make the Oral Torah useless three years after its promulgation or two hundred miles from its home base.

And this leads us to the final, most important observation: "Torah" — written and oral — is hardly a "Jewish" document. We find remarkably little attention to the "Jewishness" of the society — the victim or the injurer. On the contrary, the frame of reference is not only neutral as to a particular place or time, it is also indifferent to the "ethnic origin" of the participants. It speaks of society, time, man and woman, family, home, and metaphysical world without stressing the particularity or ethnic distinctiveness of the individuals who form the society and demarcate the time. What is most distinctive about Judaism is the belief in the dual revelation, written and Oral Torah, yet when we come to the substance of that dual revelation, we find ourselves in a world of universals, not of the particular and distinctively Jewish at all.

THE TALMUD

Now let us turn to the second component of the Oral Torah, the commentaries to the Mishnah, which explain the meaning and significance of Mishnah's law. The great and authoritative commentary to the Mishnah is the *Gemara*, which also is simply called the *Talmud*. This is a compilation of materials relevant to a given paragraph of Mishnah, developed from the third through the fifth centuries C.E.. In point of fact, two Talmuds exist for the same Mishnah, one edited in Palestine, called the Palestinian or Jerusalem Talmud, the other edited in Babylonia, and called (naturally) the Babylonian Talmud. It is the latter that is widely studied to this day and which supplies the authoritative interpretation of Mishnah.

What is the Talmud's problem in interpretation of the Mishnah we have just read, regarding the laws or civil damages?

It is the obvious one: How do we link the Oral Torah, which assumes we pay monetary damages for personal injury, to the Written Torah, which is clear that we punish personal injury by inflicting an equivalent injury, *an eye for an eye*. We read the passage in Dr. Kirzner's translation (pp. 474-480). I have inserted his footnotes into the text of the translation, in brackets.

> Why [pay compensation]? Does the Divine Law not say "Eye for eye"? [Exod. 21:24] Why not take this literally to mean [putting out] the eye [of the offender]?

The Talmud begins with the obvious question. It asks why Mishnah ignores the Scriptural law.

> Let this not enter your mind, since it has been taught: You might think that where he put out his eye, the offender's eye should be put out, or where he cut off his arm, the offender's arm should be cut off, or again where he broke his leg, the offender's leg should be broken. [Not so; for] it is laid down, "He that smiteth any man . . ." "And he that smiteth a beast . . . ." [Lev. 24:18, 21] Just as in the case of smiting a beast compensation is to be paid, so also in the case of smiting a man compensation is to be paid [but no resort to Retaliation].

The first proof is before us. Scripture refers to smiting a beast, and, if you look up the relevant passage, you will see that Scripture then says you pay monetary damages. The passage

similarly refers to injuring a person. It follows that Scripture has
in mind the payment of monetary damages in both cases. But
this proof may not please everyone. So we are given another —
and another, and another. That is to say, virtually every
conceivable argument in behalf of monetary damages instead of
physical retaliation is going to be laid before us.

> And should this [reason] not satisfy you, note that it is
> stated, *"Moreover ye shall take no ransom for the life of
> a murderer, that is guilty of death"* [Num. 35:31],
> implying that it is only for the life of a murderer that
> you may not take *"satisfaction"* [i.e., ransom, and thus
> release him from capital punishment], whereas you may
> take *"satisfaction"* [even] for the principal limbs,
> though these cannot be restored.

The second proof depends upon a close reading of the cited
passage. The Scripture says you do not take a ransom — a
monetary payment — for the life of a murderer. This is then
turned around. For the life of a murderer, you may not take a
ransom, but you do so for the destruction of limbs.

> How [do you know that it refers] to pecuniary compen-
> sation? Why not say that it really means capital punish-
> ment? [As indeed appears from the literal meaning of
> the text.]
>   Let not this enter your mind; first, because it is
> compared to the case dealt with in the text, "He that
> smiteth a beast mortally shall make it good," and
> furthermore, because it is written soon after, "as he
> hath done so shall it be done to him" [Lev. 24:19] thus
> proving that it means pecuniary compensation.
>   But what is meant by the statement, "If this reason
> does not satisfy you"? [Why should it not satisfy you?]
> The difficulty which further occurred to the Tanna
> [Mishnah-teacher] was as follows: What is your reason
> for deriving the law of man injuring man from the law
> of smiting a beast and not from the law governing the
> case of killing man [where retaliation is the rule]?

This is the right question. We have now reviewed two proofs.

Both of them in one way or another depend upon the analogy between man and beast. But perhaps such an analogy is false. This is the answer.

> I would answer: It is proper to derive [the law of] injury [Lev. 24:19] from [the law governing another case of] injury [i.e., where man injured beast], and not to derive [the law of] injury [Lev. 24:19] from [the law governing the case of] murder.
>
> It could, however, be argued to the contrary; [that it is proper] to derive [the law of injury inflicted upon] man from [another case of] man but not to derive [the law of injury inflicted upon] man from [the case of] beast. This was the point of the statement, "If, however, this reason does not satisfy you."
>
> [The answer is as follows:] 'It is stated: *Moreover ye shall take no ransom for the life of a murderer who is guilty of death; but he shall surely be put to death*, implying that it was only *'for the life of a murderer'* that you may not take ransom whereas you may take ransom [even] *for* principal *limbs* though these cannot be restored . . .'

We have concluded that line of argument. But the topic is not finished. We now turn to the matter afresh, as if nothing had been said.

> . . . . It was taught: R. Dosthai b. Judah says: *"Eye for eye* means pecuniary compensation." You say pecuniary compensation, but perhaps it is not so, but actual retaliation [by putting out an eye] is meant?
>
> What then will you say where the eye of one was big and the eye of the other little, for how can I in this case apply the principle of eye for eye? If, however, you say that in such a case pecuniary compensation will have to be taken, did not the Torah state, *Ye shall have one manner of law* [Lev. 24:22], implying that the manner of law should be the same in all cases?
>
> I might rejoin: What is the difficulty even in that case? Why not perhaps say that for eyesight taken away the Divine Law ordered eyesight to be taken away from

the offender? [Without taking into consideration the sizes of the respective eyes.]

For if you will not say this, how could capital punishment be applied in the case of a dwarf killing a giant or a giant killing a dwarf [where the bodies of the murderer and the murdered are not alike], seeing that the Torah says, *Ye shall have one manner of law,* implying that the manner of law should be the same in all cases, unless you say that for a life taken away the Divine Law ordered the life of the murderer to be taken away?"

We have a quite new argument. Scripture cannot possibly have meant that we exact physical retaliation, for what if that is not possible? Clearly it is possible to pay damages. So the original intention of the Mosaic Law must be to impose monetary compensation, not to make the blinding of a person the appropriate punishment for damaging another's eye.

R. Simeon b. Yohai says, *"Eye for eye"* means pecuniary compensation. You say pecuniary compensation, but perhaps it is not so, but actual retaliation [by putting out an eye] is meant? What then will you say where a blind man put out the eye of another man, or where a cripple cut off the hand of another, or where a lame person broke the leg of another?

How can I carry out in this case [the principle of retaliation of] *"eye for eye,"* seeing that the Torah says, *Ye shall have one manner of law,* implying that the manner of law should be the same in all cases?

I might rejoin: What is the difficulty even in this case? Why not perhaps say that it is only where it is possible [to carry out the principle of retaliation that] it is to be carried out, whereas where it is impossible, it is impossible, and the offender will have to be released altogether.

For if you will not say this, what could be done in the case of a person afflicted with a fatal organic disease killing a healthy person.

You must therefore admit that it is only where it is possible [to resort to the law of retaliation] that it is

> resorted to, whereas where it is impossible, it is impossible, and the offender will have to be released.
>
> .... Abbaye said: [The principle of pecuniary compensation] could be derived from the teaching of the School of Hezekiah. For the School of Hezekiah taught: "Eye for eye, life for life" [Exod. 21:24], but not *"life and eye for eye."*
>
> Now if you assume that actual retaliation is meant, it could sometimes happen that eye and life would be taken for eye, as while the offender is being blinded, his soul might depart from him.

This is a good argument. We really cannot exact only an eye for an eye. We might end up taking the person's life. But the Talmud does not accept every assertion, nor does it heed even the great authority behind a given saying. There is a perfectly good answer, which we shall now hear.

> But what difficulty is this? Perhaps what it means is that we have to form an estimate [whether the offender would stand the operation or not], and only if the offender will be able to stand it will retaliation be adopted, but if he will not be able to stand it, retaliation will not be adopted? And if after we estimate that he would be able to stand it and execute retaliation it so happens that his spirit departs from him, [there is nobody to blame,] as if he dies, let him die.

The answer is fair. If the person seems able to take the punishment, we give it to him or her.

We see not one *midrash* or two, but a whole series of explanations and interpretations to link the written and oral Torah. Clearly, every sort of proof is going to be adduced, lest a single argument fail to forge the necessary link between the one and the other. The issue is not whether we are persuaded, though some may find that the original meaning of Scripture was exactly what the later rabbis allege. The issue is how we are to understand the relationship between the one Torah and the other. The answer is supplied by the various rabbis, who flourished over a period of five centuries.

We also observe the skepticism of the anonymous "voice"

who speaks throughout. Every argument is tested, every
contrary point is introduced. There is no "faith" demanded
here, only the constant exercise of reason. The Talmud is a
document of careful, critical thinking. The rabbis are men who
take nothing on faith, who doubt, and doubt again. "Is the term
smiting actually mentioned?" "How do you know that it refers
to . . ." "If this reason does not satisfy you, why whould it not
satisfy you? The difficulty which further occurred . . ." And so
on throughout. The flow of argument, as it were, is against the
assertion of fact. Let us now generalize and ask how the minds
of the rabbis work, what are the modes of thought characteristic of Talmudic or Rabbinic Judaism as revealed in the
passage of Talmud we have read.

The Talmudic Mode of Thought

Talmudic thinking is characterized by the persistence of the
spirit of criticism in four modes: (1) abstract, rational criticism
of each tradition in sequence and of the answers hazarded to
the questions; (2) historical criticism of sources and their
(un)harmonious relationship; (3) philological and literary criticism of the meanings of words and phrases; and (4) practical
criticism of what people actually do in order to carry out their
religious obligations.

It goes without saying that these four modes of criticism
are peculiarly contemporary. Careful, skeptical examination of
answers posed to problems is utterly commonplace to modern
men and women. Historical criticism of sources, which does not
gullibly accept whatever is alleged as fact, is the beginning of
historical study. Philological study of the origins and meanings
of words, literary criticism of the style of expression — these are
familiar. Finally, we take for granted that it is normal to
examine people's actions against some large principle of
behavior. These are traits of inquiry that are both talmudic and
routinely modern.

What makes them different from modern modes of
thought? It is the remarkable claim that in the give and take of
argument, in the processes of criticism, you do something
transcendent, more than this-worldly. I cannot overemphasize
how remarkable is the combination of rational criticism and the

supernatural value attached to it. You simply cannot understand Rabbinic Judaism without confronting this other-worldly context. The claim is that in seeking reason and order, you serve God. But what are we to make of that claim? Does lucid thinking bring heavenly illumination? How can people suggest so?

Perhaps the best answer may be sought in our own experience. Whence comes insight? Having put everything together in a logical and orderly way, we sometimes find ourselves immobilized. We sometimes catch an unexpected insight and come in some mysterious way to a comprehension of a whole which exceeds the sum of its parts. And we cannot explain how we have seen what, in a single instant, stuns us by its ineluctable fittingness — by unearned insight, inexplicable understanding. For the rabbis that stunning moment of rational insight comes with *siyyata dishamaya*, the help of Heaven. The charisma imparted by the rabbinic imagination to the brilliant scholar is not different in substance from the moral authority and spiritual dignity imparted by contemporary intellectuals to the great minds of the age. The profound honor to be paid to the intellectual paragons — the explorers of the unknown, the men and women with courage to doubt the accepted truths of the hour — is not much different from the deference shown by the disciple to the rabbi. So the religious experience of the rabbi and the secular experience of the intellectual differ not in quality. They gravely differ in the ways by which we explain and account for that experience. Still, in reflecting upon the commonalities of experience, we are enabled to enter into the curious mode of religiosity discovered within the Talmud. That accounts for our capacity to follow the primary question of the Talmud: Why are things as we suppose they are? Perhaps they are just the opposite.

The persistent issue is, What is the reason for a ruling? Once reasons are adduced, they may be criticized and replaced. Changing situations may produce new reasons and end the pertinence of old ones. Just as the argument moves from point to point, so it remains open-ended. Not only new data, but also new intelligence and ideas may be introduced to change the course of the legal discussion. Thus the editors of the Talmud have turned materials of merely historical interest and authority into a living and vigorous discussion of wholly contemporary concern, vivid as long as the living choose to engage their minds with the ideas and the reasoning of the long dead.

It must have taken considerable courage to criticize an authoritative law code, the Mishnah. It would have been pious merely to accept those laws and digest them for future generations to memorize and copy. Judah the Patriarch, who promulgated the Mishnah, was called "our holy rabbi"; he and those whose traditions he organized and handed on were very ancient authorities. Two or three centuries later the prestige of the Mishnah, regarded, as we saw, as the "Oral Torah" revealed by Moses at Sinai, was considerable. To ask for reasons, to criticize those reasons, to seek contradictions, to add to the law, to revise or even reject what the ancients had said — these were acts of scholars who had no equivalent claim either to firsthand knowledge of the Oral Torah or to the sanctity and prestige of the Tanniam. Yet that is exactly what the Amoraim, who commented on the Mishnah, did. And they did so in such a way as to revise everything that had gone before, to place upon the whole heritage of the past the indelible and distinct, unmistakable stamp of their own minds.

The Amoraim did not confuse respect with servility; they carefully nurtured the disciples' critical and creative faculties. Gibbon said (probably unfairly) of the Byzantine schools, "Not a single composition of history, philosophy, or literature has been saved from oblivion by the intrinsic beauties of style, or sentiment, or original fancy, or even of successful imitation." By contrast, the Babylonian Talmud is the product not of servility to the past or of dogmatism in the present, but of an exceptionally critical, autonomous rationalism and an utterly independent spirit. The Amoraim gave a cool reception to pedantry. Clearly, to them mere learning was insufficient. Not what scholars knew, but what they could do with what they knew was decisive. The authority and approbation of the elders were set aside by the critical accomplishments of the newest generation. In the fullest sense, the Amoraim were not traditionalists. They took the laws and traditions of the early generations into their care, respectfully learning them, reverently handing them on, but their rational wisdom and unrelenting criticism were wholly their own.

The Talmud is a fundamentally nonhistorical, nontraditional document. It does not appeal to the authority of the past. The elegant structures of debate are not assigned to specific authorities, because to the Talmud the time and place, name and occupation of the authority behind an inquiry are of no great interest. Logic and criticism are not bound to specific historical or biographical circumstances. Therefore, the principles of an orderly, disciplined, holy way of life are not reduced to the personalities or situations of the promulgators.

Talmudic thinking stands over against historical and psychological interpretation because of its preference for finding abstraction and order in concrete, perennial problems of daily life. What counts is reason — ubiquitous, predominant, penetrating. The object of reason is twofold: first, the criticism of the given by the criterion of fundamental principles of order; and second, the demonstration of the presence within commonplace matters of transcendent considerations. Casuistical controversy over trivialities does not always link up to a transcendent concern for the sacred; but it always is meant to. For the ultimate issue is how to discover the order of the well-ordered existence and well-correlated relationships; the prevalent attitude is perfect seriousness (not specious solemnity) about life, people's intentions, and their actions.

The talmudic approach to life presupposes that order is better than chaos, reflection than whim, decision than accident, and ratiocination and rationality than witlessness and force. The only admissible force is the power of fine logic, ever refined against the discipline of everyday life. The rabbis' effort is to pattern the relationships among people so that all things are intelligible, well-regulated, trustworthy — and sanctified. The Talmud stands for the perfect intellectualization of life, that is, the subjection of life to rational study. For nothing is so trivial as to be unrelated to some conceptual, abstract principle. If the placing of a napkin or the washing of the hands is subject to critical analysis, what can be remote from the Talmud's rigorous inquiry? But the mode of inquiry is not exclusively human. A human being is made in God's image, and that part which is like God is not corporeal. It is the thing which separates man and woman from beast: the mind, consciousness. When we use our minds, we act like God. That surely is a conviction uncharacteristic of modern intellectuals, yet at the heart of Talmudic intellectuality.

The Talmud's conception of us is obvious: We think,

therefore we and what we do are worth taking seriously. We will respond to reason and subject ourselves to discipline founded upon criticism. Our response will consist in self-consciousness about all we do, think, and say. To be sure, the human being is dual; we are twin-things, ready to do evil and ready to do good. But readiness is not all; beyond it is mindfulness. As the Talmudic warning about not interrupting one's study even to admire a tree — that is, nature — makes clear, we cannot afford even for one instant to break off from consciousness, to open ourselves to what appears then to be "natural"; to be mindless is to lose touch with revealed order and revealed law, the luminous disciplines of the sacred.

The Talmud's single-minded pursuit of unifying truths itself constitutes its primary discipline. But the discipline does not derive from the perception of unifying order in the natural world. It comes, rather, from the lessons imparted supernaturally in the Torah. The sages perceive the Torah not as a mélange of sources and laws of different origins, but as a single, unitary document, a corpus of laws reflective of an underlying, ordered will. The Torah reveals the way things should be, just as the rabbis' formulation and presentation of their laws tell how things should be, whether or not that is how they actually are done. The order derives from the plan and will of the Creator of the world, the foundation of all reality. As we saw, the Torah was interpreted by the talmudic rabbis to be the architect's design for reality: God looked into the Torah and created the world, just as an architect follows his prior design in raising a building. A single, whole Torah — in two forms, oral and written, to be sure — underlies the one, seamless reality of the world. The search for the unities hidden by the pluralities of the trivial world, the supposition that some one thing is revealed by many things — these represent in intellectual form the theological and metaphysical conception of a single, unique God, creator of heaven and earth, revealer of one complete Torah, guarantor of the unity and ultimate meaning of all the human actions and events that constitute history. On that account the Talmud links the private human deeds to a larger pattern, and provides a large and general "meaning" for small, particular, trivial doings.

Behind this conception of the unifying role of reason and the integrating force of criticism lies the conviction that God supplies the model for the human mind; therefore a human being, through reasoning in the Torah's laws, may penetrate God's intent and plan. The rabbis of the Talmud believed they studied Torah as God did in heaven; their schools were conducted like the academy on high. They performed rites just as God performed rites, wearing fringes as did he, putting on phylacteries just as did God. In studying Torah they besought the heavenly paradigm revealed by God "in his image" and handed down from Moses and the prophets to their own teachers. If the rabbis of the Talmud studied and realized the divine teaching of Moses, whom they called "our rabbi," it was because the order they would impose upon earthly affairs would replicate on earth the order they perceived from heaven, the rational construction of reality. It is Torah which reveals the mind of God, the priniciples by which he shaped reality. So studying Torah is not merely imitating God, who does the same, but is a way to the apprehension of God and the attainment of the sacred. The modes of argument are holy because they lead from earth to heaven, as prayer or fasting or self-denial cannot. Reason is the way, God's way, and the holy human being is therefore one who is able to think clearly and penetrate profoundly into the mysteries of the Torah and, especially, of its so very trivial laws. In context those trivialities contain revelation.

The talmudic way of thinking appeals to, and itself approves, the cultured over the uncultured, those capable of self-conscious criticism over those too dull to think. "An ignorant man cannot be pious." Fear of sin without wisdom is worthless. The sages encouraged the articulate over the inarticulate: "The shy person cannot learn." For the give-and-take of argument, one cannot hang back out of feigned or real bashfulness. Reason makes people equals and reveals their inequalities. Reason is not a quirk of personality, but a trait of mind, therefore, it must be shamelessly and courageously drawn out.

What is talmudic in thinking is perpetual skepticism, expressed in response to every declarative sentence or affirmative statement. Once one states that matters are so, it is inevitable that he will find as a response: "Why do you think so?" or "Perhaps things are the opposite of what you say?" or "How can you say so when a contrary principle may be adduced?" Articulation, forthrightness, subtle reasoning expressed lucidly, skepticism — these are the traits of intellectuals, not of untrained and undeveloped minds, nor of neat scholars, capable only to serve as curators of the past, not as critics of the present.

Above all, talmudic thinking rejects gullibility and credulity. It is, indeed, peculiarly modern in its systematic skepticism, its testing of each proposition, not to destroy, but to refine, what people suppose to be so. As we have seen time and again, the Talmud's first question is not "*Who* says so?" but "Why?" In the talmudic approach to thought, faith is restricted to ultimate matters, to the fundamental principles of reality beyond which one may not penetrate. Akabya, an early talmudic authority, wanted to try to find out whence one comes and whither one is going. The answers will yield humility. But humility in the face of ultimate questions is not confused with servility before the assertions, the truth-claims, of putative authorities, ancient or modern, who are no more than mortal.

Since the harvest of learning is humility, however, the more one seeks to find out, the greater will be one's virtue. And the way to deeper perception lies in skepticism about shallow assertion. One must place as small a stake as possible in the acceptance of specific allegations. The fewer vested convictions, the greater the chances for wide-ranging inquiry. But while modern skepticism may yield — at least in the eye of its critics — corrosive and negative results, talmudic skepticism produces measured, restrained, and limited insight. The difference must be in the open-endedness of the talmudic inquiry; nothing is ever left as a final answer, a completed solution. The fruit of insight is inquiry; the results of inquiry is insight, in endless progression. The only road closed is the road back, to the unarticulated, the unconscious, and the unselfconscious. For once consciousness is achieved and a reason spelled out, one cannot again pretend there is no reason, that nothing has been articulated. For the Talmud the alternatives are not faith or nihilism, but reflection or dumb reflex, consciousness or animal instinct. Humankind, in God's image, has the capacity to reflect and to criticize. All an animal can do is act and respond. And a human being may be holy or unholy. An animal can only be clean or unclean — a considerable difference.

In short, the Talmud is a document created by the intellect devoted to morality and seeking sanctity. It takes for granted that people's primary capacity is to think; they therefore are to be taken with utmost seriousness. The Talmud endures as a monument to intellectualism focused upon the application of practical rationality to society. It pays tribute, on every page, to the human potential to think morally, yet without lachrymose sentimentality; to reflect about fundamentals and basic principles, yet for concrete purposes and with ordinary society in mind. The good, well-regulated society will nurture disciplined, strong character. The mighty human being — "one who overcomes his impulses" — will stand as a pillar of the good society. This is what I understand as the result of the intellectual activity of the moral intellect. Reason, criticism, restraint, and rational exchange of ideas — these are not data for the history of talmudic literature alone. The Talmud itself testifies to their necessary consequences for the personality and for society alike.

The Religious Beliefs of Judaism: God and Israel

We have examined the method of Rabbinic Judaism, its modes of thinking, its ways of deriving religious beliefs and conceptions, and its centrality of Torah study. It is time to ask about the substance of Rabbinic Judaism, its conceptions of God and humankind, history and eternity, Israel — the Jewish people — and the nations.

One must first ask, How do we find these conceptions? Where do we locate them? Do we have now to consider two thousand years of theological writings, the decrees of councils of rabbis, or the conceptions of philosophers and authoritative theologians?

The answer is negative. The best place in which to discover and study the religious beliefs of Judaism is in the Jewish prayerbook, the *Siddur*, a document of public piety. In its main outlines, it begins with Rabbinic Judaism but in its contents, it goes back to still more ancient times. As we shall see, the Siddur contains descriptions and interpretations of Judaism's view of the world.

When we adduce these conceptions in the Siddur, we may be certain we are describing religious beliefs held not by a few brilliant religious geniuses, rabbis, theologians, or philosophers, but by everyone who turned, in the humility of his or her heart, to God. For the Siddur is the document of piety characteristic of, believed in, shared and understood by the masses of Jews, not merely by the religious elite. To be sure, it may be the creation of the religious virtuosi, but it speaks to and for the common folk. That is why we may confidently describe the religious beliefs of Judaism out of the materials of worship; materials which, we shall observe, contain and express simultaneously a vast conception of reality, and a detailed and humble interpretation of everyday affairs.

God

The great teaching, the dogma, of Rabbinic Judaism — as of all forms of Judaism throughout history — is that God is one. That is not meant as a philosophical declaration, alleging the unity of the Divinity as against the claim of the plurality of Divinity; it is a religious affirmation, to be discerned from the language of the prayer. It is to this majestic proclamation of faith that we now turn.

Evening and morning, the pious Jew proclaims the unity and uniqueness of God. The proclamation is preceded and followed by blessings. The whole constitutes the credo of the Judaic tradition. It is "what the Jews believe." Components recur everywhere. Let us first examine the prayer, called *Shema*, "Hear."

The *Shema* begins with a celebration of God as creator of the world. In the morning, one says,

Praised are You, O Lord our God, King of the universe.
You fix the cycles of light and darkness;
You ordain the order of all creation.
You cause light to shine over the earth;
Your radiant mercy is upon its inhabitants.
In Your goodness the work of creation
Is continually renewed day by day . . .

> O cause a new light to shine on Zion;
> May we all soon be worthy to behold its radiance.
> Praised are You, O Lord, Creator of the heavenly bodies.

The corresponding prayer in the evening refers to the setting of the sun:

> Praised are You . . .
> Your command brings on the dusk of evening.
> Your wisdom opens the gates of heaven to a new day.
> With understanding You order the cycles of time;
> Your will determines the succession of seasons;
> You order the stars in their heavenly courses.
> You create day, and You create night,
> Rolling away light before darkness . . .
> Praised are You, O Lord, for the evening dusk.

Morning and evening, the Jew responds to the natural order of the world with thanks and praise of God who created the world and who actively guides the daily events of nature. Whatever happens in nature gives testimony to the sovereignty of the creator. And that testimony is not in unnatural disasters, but in the most ordinary events, sunrise and sunset. These, especially, evoke the religious response.

For the Jew, God is not merely creator, but purposeful creator. The works of creation serve to justify — to testify to Torah — the revelation of Sinai. Torah is the mark not merely of divine sovereignty, but of divine grace and love, source of life here and now and in eternity. So goes the second blessing:

> Deep is Your love for us, O Lord our God;
> Bounteous is Your compassion and tenderness.
> You taught our fathers the laws of life.
> And they trusted in You, Father and King.
> For their sake be gracious to us, and teach us,
> That we may learn Your laws and trust in You.
> Father, merciful Father, have compassion upon us;
> Endow us with discernment and understanding.
> Grant us the will to study Your Torah,
> To heed its words and to teach its precepts . . .
> Enlighten our eyes in Your Torah,

Open our hearts to Your commandments . . .
Unite our thoughts with singleness of purpose
To hold You in reverence and in love . . .
You have drawn us close to You;
We praise You and thank You in truth.
With love do we thankfully proclaim Your unity,
And praise You who chose Your people Israel in love.

Here is the way in which revelation takes concrete and specific form in the Judaic tradition; God, the creator, revealed his will for creation through the Torah, given to Israel his people. That Torah contains the "laws of life."

The Jew, moved to worship by the daily "miracle" of sunrise and sunset, responds with the prayer that he or she, like nature, may enjoy divine compassion. But what does that compassion consist of? The ability to understand, and the will to study *Torah*!

This is the mark of the relationship between God and humankind, and Jewish man and woman in particular, that a person's eyes are open to Torah and that his or her heart is open to the commandments. These are the means of divine service, of reverence and love for God. Israel sees itself as "chosen," close to God, because of Torah, and it finds its devotion to Torah the mark of its chosenness. The covenant made at Sinai, a contract on Israel's side to do and hear the Torah, on God's side to be the God of Israel — that covenant is evoked by natural events, then confirmed by human deeds and devotion.

Torah, revelation, leads Jews to enunciate the chief teaching of revelation:

Hear O Israel, the Lord our God, the Lord is One.

This proclamation is followed by three Scriptural passages. First, Deuteronomy 6:4-9:

You shall love the Lord your God with all your heart, with all your soul, with all your might.

And further, one must diligently teach the children these words and talk of them everywhere and always, and place them on one's forehead, doorposts, and gates.

The second Scripture is Deuteronomy 11:13-21, which emphasizes that if the people keep the commandments, they will enjoy worldly blessings, but if they do not, they will be punished and disappear from the good land God gives them.

The third is Numbers 15:37-41, the commandment to wear fringes on the corners of one's garments, today attached to the prayer shawl worn at morning services. The fringes remind the Jew of *all* the commandments of the Lord.

The proclamation is completed, yet remains open-ended, for having created humankind and told them His will, God is not unaware of events since Sinai. The human being is frail, and in the contest between the word of God and the will of man and woman, Torah is not always the victor. Humankind inevitably falls short of what is asked of them, and Jews know that their own history consists of divine punishment for human failure time and again. The theme of redemption, therefore, is introduced.

Redemption, the third element in the tripartite world view, resolves the tension between what people are told to do and what they are able actually to accomplish. In the end it is the theme of God not as creator or revealer, but God as redeemer, that concludes the twice daily drama:

> You are our King and our father's King,
> Our redeemer and our father's redeemer.
> You are our creator . . .
> You have ever been our redeemer and deliverer
> There can be no God but You . . .
> You, O Lord our God, rescued us from Egypt;
> You redeemed us from the house of bondage . . .
> You split apart the waters of the Red Sea,
> The faithful You rescued, the wicked drowned . . .
> Then Your beloved sang hymns of thanksgiving . . .
> They acclaimed the King, God on high,
> Great and awesome source of all blessings,
> The everliving God, exalted in His majesty.
> He humbles the proud and raises the lowly;
> He helps the needy and answers His people's call . . .
> Then Moses and all the children of Israel
> Sang with great joy this song to the Lord:
> Who is like You O Lord among the mighty?

Who is like You, so glorious in holiness?
So wondrous Your deeds, so worthy of praise!
The redeemed sang a new song to You;
They sang in chorus at the shore of the sea,
Acclaiming Your sovereignty with thanksgiving:
The Lord shall reign for ever and ever.
Rock of Israel, arise to Israel's defense!
Fulfill Your promise to deliver Judah and Israel.
Our redeemer is the Holy One of Israel,
The Lord of hosts is His name.
Praised are You, O Lord, redeemer of Israel.

Redemption is both in the past and in the future. That God not only creates but also redeems is attested by Israel's redemption from Egyptian bondage. The congregation repeats the exultant song of Moses and the people at the Red Sea, not as scholars making a learned allusion, but as participants in the salvation of old and of time to come. Then the people turn to the future and ask that Israel once more be redeemed.

But redemption is not only past and future. When the needy are helped, when the proud are humbled and the lowly are raised — in such commonplace, daily events, redemption is already present. Just as creation is not only in the beginning, but occurs daily, so redemption is not only at the Red Sea, but every day, in humble events. Just as revelation was not at Sinai alone, but takes place whenever people study Torah, whenever God opens their hearts to the commandments, so redemption and creation are daily events.

The great cosmic events of creation in the beginning, redemption at the Red Sea, revelation at Sinai — these are everywhere, every day near at hand. The Rabbinic Jew views secular reality under the mythic aspect of eternal, ever-recurrent events. Whatever happens to the individual and to the world, whether good or evil, falls into the pattern revealed of old and made manifest each day. Historical events produce a framework into which future events will find a place, by which they will be understood. Nothing that happens cannot be subsumed by the paradigm.

We began by saying that the *Shema* proclaims "the unity of God." When, however, we reflect upon the language of the *Shema*, we realize that that unity which is affirmed is the oneness of nature and history, the conviction that all reality is the creation of God and finds unity in the oneness of the Creator. You recall that we have already alluded to the sense of order and meaning that underlies the Talmudic mode of thinking. Now you realize that the mode of thinking is an effect, something produced by a fundamental and all-encompassing conception of being. That conception is thus expressed: Above all things, behind all things, is the one God who made heaven and earth, who regulates nature and history. The rising and the setting of the sun testify to the oneness, the orderliness of creation. The Torah contains and expresses the orderliness of human history. Redemption, at the end of days, will complete the unity of being.

Before we leave the conception of God as creator, revealer, and redeemer, let us turn to one more liturgy in which this trilogy is expressed. Recited on the Days of Awe, the prayer expresses God's sovereignty, remembrance, and redemption.

The Days of Awe, sometimes called "the high holy days," are the New Year, *Rosh Hashanah*, and the Day of Atonement, *Yom Kippur*. These come in the autumn, normally in September. They focus not upon the community so much as upon the life of the individual, his or her destiny in the coming year, and the atonement for deeds done in the year now ending.

On the New Year, three great themes of the Judaic tradition, creation, revelation, and redemption, are expressed in a triplet of prayers on the themes of God's rule, as expressed through revelation; God's remembrance, beginning with the recollection of his creation of the world; and his coming redemption of humankind at the sound of the *shofar*, or ram's horn. Each of these prayers is concluded with the dramatic sound of the *shofar*.

> *God reigns.*
>
> We worship no earthly power. Only to the only King do we bow and kneel, as a sign of ultimate loyalty to Him alone, and awareness of our mortality.
>
> We rise to our duty to praise the Lord of all, to acclaim the Creator. He made our lot unlike that of other people, assigning us a unique destiny.
>
> We bend the knee and bow, proclaiming Him as King of kings, the Holy One praised be He. He unfurled the

heavens and established the earth. His throne of glory is in the heavens above, His majestic Presence in the loftiest heights. He and no other is God, our faithful King. So we are told in His Torah: "Remember now and always that the Lord is God in heaven and on earth. There is no other."

And so we hope in You, Lord our God, soon to see Your splendor, sweeping idolatry away so that false gods will be utterly destroyed, perfecting earth by Your kingship so that all mankind will invoke Your name, bringing all the earth's wicked back to You, repentant. Then all who live will know that to You every knee must bend, every tongue pledge loyalty. To You, Lord, may all men bow in worship, may they give honor to Your glory. May everyone accept the rule of Your kingship. Reign over all, soon and for all time. Sovereignty is Yours in glory, now and forever.

Our God and God of our fathers, cause Your sovereignty to be acknowledged throughout the world. May Your splendor and dignity be reflected in the lives of all who dwell on earth. Then all creatures will know that You created them, all living things will comprehend that You gave them life, everything that breathes will proclaim: The Lord God of Israel is King, and His dominion embraces all.

Our God and God of our fathers, . . . make our lives holy with Your commandments and let Your Torah be our portion. Fill our lives with Your goodness, and gladden us with Your triumph . . . Cleanse our hearts to serve You faithfully, for You are faithful and Your word endures forever. Praised are You, Lord, King of all the earth who sanctifies . . . the people Israel and the Day of Remembrance.

Today the world is born. Today all creatures everywhere stand in judgment, some as children and some as slaves. If we merit consideration as children, show us a father's mercy. If we stand in judgment as slaves, grant us freedom. We look to You for compassion when You declare our fate, awesome, holy God.

God remembers.

Creation You remember, Lord, considering the deeds of all mankind from ancient days. All thoughts are revealed to You, all secrets since the beginning of time. For You there is no forgetting, from You nothing is hidden. You remember every deed, You know every doer. You know all things, Lord our God, and foresee events to the end of time. You have set a day for bringing to judgment countless human beings and their infinite deeds. This You ordained from the beginning, this You made known from of old.

This day is the birthday of Creation, a reminder of the first day. Its observance is a law for the House of Jacob, ordained by the God of our fathers. And this is a day of decree for all nations: war or peace, famine or abundance. Every single creation stands in judgment: life or death. Who is not called to account on this day? The record of every human being is set before You, his work and his ways, his designs and his desires.

Blessed is the man who forgets You not, who draws courage from You. Those who seek You shall not stumble, those who trust You shall not be disgraced when the record of all deeds is set before You and You probe every man's deeds. Remember us as You remembered Noah in love, graciously saving him when You released the flood to destroy all creatures because of their evil deeds. You made his descendants numerous as the dust of the earth, as the sand of the sea.

Our God and God of our fathers, remember us favorably, grant us merciful deliverance for our sake, remember Your loving kindness and Your covenant with Abraham our father on Mount Moriah. Recall how Abraham subdued his compassion to do Your will whole-heartedly, binding his son Isaac on the altar; subdue Your wrath with Your compassion. In Your great goodness favor Your people, Your city and Your inheritance. Fulfill for us the promise contained in Your Torah transmitted by Moses: "For their sake I will remember the covenant with their ancestors whom I

brought out of the land of Egypt in the sight of the
nations, to be their God. I am the Lord." (Lev. 26:45)

You remember all things forgotten; for You there is
no forgetting. This day in mercy remember the binding
of Isaac on behalf of his descendants. Praised are You,
Lord who remembers the covenant.

God reveals. God redeems.

You were revealed to Your holy people at Mount Sinai.
Your mysterious Presence was revealed amid clouds of
Your glory. All creation stood in awe, trembling, when
You our King did manifest Yourself, teaching our forefathers Torah and *mitzvot*. Out of flaming fire, amid
thunder and lightning, amid blasts of the *shofar* did You
reveal Yourself to them.

Thus is it written in Your Torah:

On the third day, as morning dawned at Mount Sinai,
there were peals of thunder and flashes of lightning, a
dense cloud on the mountain, and loud blasts of the
shofar; everyone in the camp trembled. The blare of
the *shofar* grew louder and louder. As Moses spoke,
God answered him in thunder. (Exod. 19:16, 19)

So sang the Psalmist:

The God of judgment ascends His throne with shouts
of acclamation; the Lord of compassion ascends with
a fanfare of the *shofar*. With trumpets and *shofar*,
acclaim the presence of the Lord our King. Sound the
shofar on the New Moon, announcing our solemn
festival. It is Israel's eternal ritual, the God of Jacob
calls us to judgment. (Ps. 47:6, 98:6, 81:4-5)

And thus proclaimed Your prophet:

All you who dwell in the world, inhabitants of the
earth, shall see when the signal of redemption is
hoisted on the mountains, and shall hear when the
shofar is sounded. (Isa. 18:3)

Our God and God of our fathers, sound the great *shofar*
for our freedom, raise high the banner to gather our
exiles. Unite our scattered people, gather our dispersed

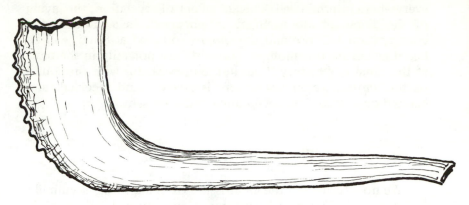

A SHOFAR (RAM'S HORN)

from the ends of the earth. Lead us with song to Zion Your city, with everlasting joy to Jerusalem Your sanctuary, where our forefathers offered their sacrifices of well-being and their burnt offerings. And thus is it written in Your Torah:

> "On your joyous occasions, your fixed festivals and new moon days, you shall sound the *trumpets* . . . They shall be a reminder of you before the Lord your God; I the Lord, am your God." (Num. 10:10)

There is none like You, hearing the *shofar* and attending to its sound. Praised are You, Lord who hears the sound of the *shofar* of His people Israel with compassion.

We have read a monumental prayer. Let us briefly review its components, in which we see the themes of creation, revelation, and redemption, just as we found the same themes in the *Shema*. First we saw the prayer proclaiming God as king. We shall come across this same prayer again in a moment. What it stresses is not only that God rules, but that, at the end of time, everyone in the world will recognize God as ruler. The prayer therefore asks that God hasten that day. The second prayer concerns God's remembering — a curiously human conception. This prayer, stressing God as creator, also introduces the theme of divine judgment on the Days of Atonement. The dominant theme here is redemption. Finally comes the prayer expressing the belief in God as revealer and redeemer — for the themes are everywhere intermingled. The actual act of revelation, the giving of the Torah at Mount Sinai, is rehearsed. In a moment the congregation will rise and the *shofar*, sounded at Sinai, will be heard again. At this moment thoughts are not only in the past, at the Sinai of "history," but in the present, for with the sound of the *shofar*, Torah once more is given — and received, and handed on — tradition, acceptance in the present.

The Individual Person

We now turn from the great issues of being to the seemingly trivial but far more relevant question: How does Rabbinic Judaism express the conditions of the individual man and woman? What prayers reveal the context of private life? And what ideals for everyday life, what interpretation of the human condition of the Jewish man and the Jewish woman, are shaped by these prayers?

The answers to these questions tell us about more than the shape and substance of Judaic piety. They tell us, too, what manner of man or woman would take shape, for the constant repetition of the sacred words and moral and ethical maxims in the setting of everyday life was bound to affect the personality and character of the individual and the quality of communal life as well. Prayer expresses the most solemn aspirations of the praying community; it is what gives that community a sense of oneness, of shared hopes; and it embodies the values of the community. But if it is the community in its single most idiomatic hour, it also presents the community at its least particular and self-aware moment, for in praying people stand before God without the mediation of ethnic consciousness. As we shall see, that does not mean in Judaic prayer one does not find an acute awareness of history and collective destiny. These are very present.

In the morning, noon, and evening prayers are found Eighteen Benedictions. Some of these, in particular at the beginning and the end, recur in Sabbath and festival prayers. But the ones reserved for everyday use are said silently. Each individual prays by and for himself or herself, but together with other silent, praying individuals. To contemplate the meaning of these prayers, one should imagine a room full of people, each alone yet in close proximity to the next, some swaying this way and that, all addressing themselves directly and intimately to God, in a whisper or in a low tone. They do not move their feet, for they are now standing before the King of kings, and it is not mete to shift and shuffle. If spoken to, they will not answer. Their attention is fixed upon the words of supplication, praise, and gratitude. When they begin, they bend their knees; so too toward the end, and at the conclusion, they step back and withdraw from the presence. These, on ordinary days, are the words they say:

Wisdom — Repentance.

You graciously endow man with intelligence;
You teach him knowledge and understanding.
Grant us knowledge, discernment, and wisdom.
Praised are You, O Lord, for the gift of knowledge.

Our Father, bring us back to Your Torah;
Our King, draw us near to Your service;
Lead us back to You truly repentant.
Praised are You, O Lord who welcomes repentance.

Forgiveness — Redemption.

Our Father, forgive us, for we have sinned;
Our King, pardon us, for we have transgressed;
You forgive sin and pardon transgression.
Praised are You, gracious and forgiving Lord.

Behold our affliction and deliver us.
Redeem us soon for the sake of Your name,
For You are the mighty Redeemer.
Praised are You, O Lord, Redeemer of Israel.

Heal us — Bless our years.

Heal us, O Lord, and we shall be healed;
Help us and save us, for You are our glory.
Grant perfect healing for all our afflictions,
O faithful and merciful God of healing.
Praised are You, O Lord, Healer of His people.

O Lord our God! Make this a blessed year;
May its varied produce bring us happiness.

Bring blessing upon the whole earth.

Bless the year with Your abounding goodness.
Praised are You, O Lord, who blesses our years.

Gather our exiles — Reign over us.

Sound the great shofar to herald man's freedom;
Raise high the banner to gather all exiles;
Gather the dispersed from the corners of the earth.
Praised are You, O Lord, who gathers our exiles.

Restore our judges as in days of old;
Restore our counsellors as in former times;
Remove from us sorrow and anguish.
Reign over us alone with loving kindness;
With justice and mercy sustain our cause.
Praised are You, O Lord, King who loves justice.

Humble the arrogant — Sustain the righteous.

Frustrate the hopes of those who malign us;
Let all evil very soon disappear;
Let all Your enemies be speedily destroyed.
May You quickly uproot and crush the arrogant;
May You subdue and humble them in our time.
Praised are You, O Lord, who humbles the arrogant.

Let Your tender mercies, O Lord God, be stirred
For the righteous, the pious, the leaders of Israel,
Toward devoted scholars and faithful proselytes.
Be merciful to us of the house of Israel;
Reward all who trust in You;
Cast our lot with those who are faithful to You.
May we never come to despair, for our trust is in You.
Praised are You, O Lord, who sustains the righteous.

Favor Your city and Your people.

Have mercy, O Lord, and return to Jerusalem, Your city;
May Your Presence dwell there as You promised;
Rebuild it now, in our days and for all time;
Re-establish there the majesty of David Your servant.

Praised are You, O Lord, who rebuilds Jerusalem.
Bring to flower the shoot of Your servant David.
Hasten the advent of the Messianic redemption;
Each and every day we hope for Your deliverance.
Praised are You, O Lord, who assures our deliverance.

O Lord, our God, hear our cry!
Have compassion upon us and pity us;
Accept our prayer with loving favor.
You, O God, listen to entreaty and prayer.
O King, do not turn us away unanswered,
For You mercifully heed Your people's supplication.
Praised are You, O Lord, who is attentive to prayer.

O Lord, our God, favor Your people Israel;
Accept with love Israel's offering of prayer;
May our worship be ever acceptable to You.
May our eyes witness Your return in mercy to Zion.
Praised are You, O Lord, whose Presence returns to Zion.

> *Our thankfulness.*

We thank You, O Lord our God and God of our fathers,
Defender of our lives, Shield of our safety;
Through all generations we thank You and praise You.
Our lives are in Your hands, our souls in Your charge.

We thank You for the miracles which daily attend us,
For Your wonders and favor morning, noon, and night.
You are beneficent with boundless mercy and love.
From of old we have always placed our hope in You.
For all these blessings, O our King.
We shall ever praise and exalt You.

Every living creature thanks You, and praises You in truth.
O God, You are our deliverance and our help. Selah!
Praised are You, O Lord, for Your goodness and Your glory.

> *Peace and well-being.*

Grant peace and well-being to the whole house of Israel;
Give us of Your grace, Your love, and Your mercy.

Bless us all, O our Father, with the light of Your Presence.
It is Your light that revealed to us Your life-giving Torah,
And taught us love and tenderness, justice, mercy, and peace.

May it please You to bless Your people in every season,
To bless them at all times with Your gift of peace.
Praised are You, O Lord, who blesses Israel with peace.

The first two blessings pertain to intelligence. Man and woman thank God for mind: knowledge, wisdom, discernment. But knowledge is for a purpose, and the purpose is knowledge of Torah. Such discernment leads to the service of God and produces a spirit of repentance. We cannot pray without setting ourselves right with God, and that means repenting for what has separated us from God. Torah is the way to repentance, to return. So knowledge leads to Torah, Torah to repentance, and repentance to God. Logically, the next is the prayer for forgiveness. That is the sign of return. God forgives sin; he is gracious and forgiving. Once man and woman discern what they have done wrong through the guidance of Torah, they seek to be forgiven. Sin leads to affliction. Affliction stands at the beginning of the way to God; once people have taken that way, they ask for their suffering to end, they beg redemption. Man and woman ask for healing, salvation, a blessed year. Healing without prosperity means one may suffer in good health, starve (if not for long) in a robust body. So along with the prayer for healing goes the supplication for worldly comfort.

The individual's task is done. But what of the community? Health and comfort are not enough. The world is unredeemed. People are enslaved, in exile, and alienated. At the end of the day a great *shofar* will sound to herald the Messiah's coming. This is now besought. The Jewish people at prayer asks first for the proclamation of freedom, then for the ingathering of the exiles to the promised land. Establishing the Messianic kingdom, God needs also to restore a wise and benevolent government, good judges, good counsellors, loving justice.

Meanwhile, Israel, the Jewish people, finds itself maligned. Arrogant people hating Israel hate God as well. They should be humbled. And the pious and righteous, the scholars, the faithful proselytes, the whole House of Israel that trusts in God — these should be rewarded and sustained. Above all, remember Jerusalem. Rebuild the city and dwell there. Set up Jerusalem's king, David, and make him to prosper. These are the themes of the daily prayer: personal atonement, good health and good fortunes; collective redemption, freedom, the end of alienation, good government and true justice; the final and complete salvation of the land, Jerusalem, the Messiah. At the end comes the supplication that prayer may be heard and found acceptable, then an expression of thanksgiving not for what may come, but for the miracles and mercies already enjoyed morning, noon, and night. And at the end is the prayer for peace, a peace that consists of wholeness for the sacred community.

One who says such prayers does not wholly devote himself or herself to this world. True, worshippers ask for peace, health, and prosperity. But these are transient. At the same moment, they ask, in so many different ways, for eternity. They arise in the morning and speak of Jerusalem. At noon they make mention of the Messiah. In the evening they end the day with talk of the *shofar* to herald freedom and the ingathering of the exiles. Living here, in the profane, alien world, they constantly talk of going there, to the Holy Land and its perfect society. They address themselves to the end of days and the Messiah's time. The praying community above all seeks the fulfillment and end of its — and humankind's — travail.

Before we leave the study of the situation of the private person, let us again turn to the liturgy of the Days of Awe. There we find the most personal and individual prayers of all, those which express the relationship between each man and woman and God. What are the terms of that relationship? What is the spirit in which the Jew approaches God and seeks forgiveness, reconciliation, and atonement?

Throughout the Day of Atonement, the community of Israel many times confesses its sin, collective and individual, before God. It is a time of contrition and remorse, humility and self-criticism. The confession — which requires no comment — is as follows:

> Our God and God of our fathers, hear our
> prayers; do not ignore our plea.
> We are neither so brazen nor so arrogant to
> claim that we are righteous, without sin,
> for indeed we have sinned.
> We abuse, we betray, we are cruel.
> We destroy, we embitter, we falsify.

We gossip, we hate, we insult.
We jeer, we kill, we lie.
We mock, we neglect, we oppress.
We pervert, we quarrel, we rebel.
We steal, we transgress, we are unkind.
We are violent, we are wicked, we are xenophobic.
We yield to evil, we are zealots for bad causes.

We have ignored Your commandments and statutes, but it has not profited us. You are just, we have stumbled. You have acted faithfully, we have been unrighteous. What can we say to You; what can we tell You? You know everything, secret and revealed.

You know the mysteries of the universe, the secrets of everyone alive. You probe our innermost depths, You examine our thoughts and desires. Nothing escapes You, nothing is hidden from You. May it therefore be Your will, Lord our God and God of our fathers, to forgive us all our sins, to pardon all our iniquities, to grant us atonement for all our transgressions.

We have sinned against You unwillingly and willingly,
>And we have sinned against You by misusing our minds.

We have sinned against You through sexual immorality,
>And we have sinned against You knowingly and deceitfully.

We have sinned against You by wronging others,
>And we have sinned against You through prostitution.

We have sinned against You by deriding parents and teachers.
>And we have sinned against You by using violence.

We have sinned against You through foul speech,
>And we have sinned against You by not resisting the impulse to evil.

For all these sins, forgiving God, forgive us,
  pardon us, grant us atonement.
We have sinned against You by fraud and by
  falsehood.
  And we have sinned against You by scoffing.
We have sinned against You by dishonesty in
  business.
  And we have sinned against You by usurious
    interest.
We have sinned against You by idle chatter.
  And we have sinned against You by
    haughtiness.
We have sinned against You by rejecting
  responsibility,
  And we have sinned against You by plotting
    against others.
We have sinned against You by irreverence.
  And we have sinned against You by rushing to
    do evil.
We have sinned against You by false oaths,
  And we have sinned against You by breach of
    trust.

For all these sins, forgiving God, forgive us, pardon us,
grant us atonement.

Forgive us the breach of all commandments and
prohibitions, whether involving deeds or not, whether
known to us or not. The sins known to us we have
acknowledged, and those unknown to us are surely
known to You, as the Torah states, "The secret things
belong to the Lord our God, but the things that are
revealed belong to us and to our children forever, that
we may fulfill all the words of this Torah." For You
forgive and pardon the people Israel in every generation.
But for You we have no King to pardon us and to
forgive us for our sins.

Before I was born, I had no significance. And now
that I have been born, I am of equal worth. Dust am I
though I live: surely after death will I be dust. In Your
presence, I am aware of my frailty.

I am totally embarrassed and confused. May it be
Your will, Lord my God and God of my fathers, to help

me abstain from further sin. With Your great compassion wipe away the sins I have committed against
You, though not by means of suffering.

Keep me far from petty self-regard and petty pride,
from anger, impatience, despair, gossip and all bad
traits.

Let me not be overwhelmed by jealousy of others; let
others not be overwhelmed by jealousy of me. Grant me
the gift of seeing other people's merits, not their faults.

May He who brings peace to His universe bring peace
to us and to all the people Israel. And let us say: Amen.

The Family: Adam and Eve in the New Eden, Redemption in the Here and Now

We have just seen how the affairs of the individual and the
context of the community are intertwined in daily prayer. Let
us now ask for a second example of the same important
phenomenon, the linking of the private person, man or woman,
with the public life, the history of Israel, the Jewish people and
the Jewish community. For Rabbinic Judaism seeks to link the
individual to the community and to show how the private
affairs of the ordinary person reveal the inner meaning of the
public life of the entire holy community.

That example derives from the liturgy of marriage. It shows
that the most intimate occasion also is intrinsically the most
public.

Here a new family begins. Lover and beloved celebrate the
uniqueness, the privacy of their love. One should, therefore,
expect the nuptial prayer to speak of him and her, natural man
and natural woman. Yet the blessings that are said over the cup
of wine of sanctification are as follows:

> Praised are You, O Lord our God, King of the universe,
> Creator of the fruit of the vine.
> Praised are You, O Lord our God, King of the universe,
> who created all things for Your glory,
> Praised are You, O Lord our God, King of the universe,
> Creator of man.

> Praised are You, O Lord our God, King of the universe, who created man and woman in his image, fashioning woman from man as his mate, that together they might perpetuate life. Praised are You, O Lord, Creator of man.
>
> May Zion rejoice as her children are restored to her in joy. Praised are You, O Lord, who causes Zion to rejoice at her children's return.
>
> Grant perfect joy to these loving companions, as You did to the first man and woman in the Garden of Eden. Praised are You, O Lord, who grants the joy of bride and groom.
>
> Praised are You, O Lord, our God, King of the universe, who created joy and gladness, bride and groom, mirth, song, delight and rejoicing, love and harmony, peace and companionship. O Lord our God, may there ever be heard in the cities of Judah and in the streets of Jerusalem voices of joy and gladness, voices of bride and groom, the jubilant voices of those joined in marriage under the bridal canopy, the voices of young people feasting and singing. Praised are You, O Lord, who causes the groom to rejoice with his bride.

These seven blessings say nothing of private people and of their (anonymously) falling in love. Nor do they speak of the community of Israel, as one might expect on a public occasion. There are no hidden sermons, "to be loyal to the community and faithful in raising up new generations in it." Lover and beloved rather are transformed from natural to mythical figures. The blessings speak of archetypical Israel, represented here and now by the bride and groom.

Israel's history begins first with creation, the creation of the vine, symbol present in the place of the natural world. Creation is for God's glory. All things speak to nature, to the physical as much as to the spiritual, for all things were made by God, and the Hebrew prayer ends, "who formed the *Adam.*" All things glorify God; above all creation is humankind. The theme of ancient paradise is introduced by the simple choice of the word "Adam," so heavy with meaning. The myth of human creation is rehearsed: Man and woman are in God's image, together complete and whole, creators of life, "like God." Woman was fashioned from man, together with him to perpetuate life. And again, "blessed is the creator of man." We have moved, therefore, from the natural world to the archetypical realm of paradise. Before us we see not merely a man and a woman, but Adam and Eve.

But this Adam and this Eve also are Israel, children of Zion the mother, as expressed in the fifth blessing. Zion lies in ruins, her children scattered.

> If I forget you, O Jerusalem, may my right hand forget its skill . . . if I do not place Jerusalem above my greatest joy.

Adam and Eve cannot celebrate together without thought to the condition of the mother, Jerusalem. The children will one day come home. The mood is hopeful, yet sad as it was meant to be, for archaic Israel mourns as it rejoices, and rejoices as it mourns. Quickly, then, back to the happy occasion, for we do not let mourning lead to melancholy: "Grant perfect joy to the loving companions," for they are creators of a new line in mankind, the new Adam, the new Eve, and may their home be the garden of Eden. And if joy is there, then "praised are You for the joy of bride and groom."

The concluding blessing returns to the theme of Jerusalem. This time it evokes the tragic hour of Jerusalem's first destruction. When everyone had given up hope, supposing that with the end of Jerusalem had come the end of time, only Jeremiah counseled renewed hope. With the enemy at the gate, he sang of coming gladness:

> Thus says the Lord:
> In this place of which you say, "It is a waste, without man or beast," in the cities of Judah and the streets of Jerusalem that are desolate, without man or inhabitant or beast,
> There shall be heard again the voice of mirth and the voice of gladness, the voice of the bridegroom and the voice of the bride, the voice of those who sing as they bring thank-offerings to the house of the Lord . . .
> For I shall restore the fortunes of the land as at first, says the Lord. (Jer. 33:10-11)

The closing blessing is not merely a literary artifice or a learned allusion to the ancient prophet. It is rather the exultant, jubilant climax of this acted-out myth. Just as here and now there stand before us Adam and Eve, so here and now in this wedding, the olden sorrow having been rehearsed, we listen to the voice of gladness that is coming. The joy of this new creation prefigures the joy of the Messiah's coming, hope for which is very present in this hour. And when he comes, the joy then will echo the joy of bride and groom before us. Zion the bride, Israel the groom, united now as they will be reunited by the compassionate God — these stand under the marriage canopy.

In Rabbinic Judaism, who is the Jewish man and the Jewish woman? They are ordinary, natural people who hold a view of history centered upon Israel from the creation of the world to its final redemption. Political defeats of this world are transformed into eternal sorrow. The natural events of human life, here the marriage of ordinary folk, are heightened into a reenactment of Israel's life as a people. In marriage, individuals stand in the place of mythic figures, yet remain, after all, a boy and a girl. What gives their love its true meaning is the tripartite conception of creation, destruction, and redemption, here and now embodied in that love. But in the end, the sacred and secular are in physical love united.

The wedding of symbol and reality, the fusion and confusion of the two — these mark the classical Judaic experience, shaped by myths of creation, Adam and Eve, the Garden of Eden, the equally mythic memory of the this-worldly destruction of an old, unexceptional temple. Ordinary events, such as a political and military defeat or success, are changed into theological categories such as divine punishment and heavenly compassion. If religion is a "means of ultimate transformation," rendering the commonplace into the paradigmatic, changing the here and now into a moment of eternity and of eternal return, the marriage liturgy serves to exemplify what is *religious* in Judaic existence.

Israel: The Jewish People

We come, finally, to the third component — after Torah and God — in the structure of Rabbinic Judaism, the concept of *Israel*. Encompassing the Jewish people or the Jewish community, it is the society formed by Torah, governed by God's will. This is the concept which is easiest to misunderstand. For currently, quite rightly, most people understand by "Israel" the Jewish State, the State of Israel. But the term "Israel" was used for millenia before 1948, when the State was created, to refer to the Jewish people, and that term is a most central category of Judaic theology and belief. Christians will grasp its theological importance if they compare the concept of Israel to the concept of the Church, for in Judaism, "Israel" functions much as does "The Church" or "The Body of Christ" in Christianity.

We are now going to consider three religious meanings associated with the concept of Israel.

First, we ask about the most fundamental conception of "Israel," the meaning of its history, expressed by prayer. This prayer is said at Passover, the spring festival which celebrates the exodus of the Israelites from Egypt.

Second, we turn to the conception of the this-worldly history of Israel. This question is clearly important: Rabbinic Judaism attempts to create a timeless reality. But it does so in a most practical spirit, and on this earth. Rabbinic Judaism is not indifferent to what actually happens to the Jews as a group, but deeply concerned with that very matter. For this purpose we return to the Messianic theme, a subdominant motif throughout the liturgy, and reconsider prayers we have already examined in another context.

Third, we ask about the importance of the Land of Israel and of Jerusalem and read the Grace after Meals which links Land and Holy City to history and Messiah.

At the festival of Passover, in the spring, Jewish families gather around their tables for a holy meal. There they retell the story of the Exodus from Egypt in times long past. With unleavened bread and sanctified wine, they celebrate the liberation of slaves from Pharoah's bondage. How do they see themselves?

> We were the slaves of Pharaoh in Egypt; and the Lord our God brought us forth from there with a mighty hand and an outstretched arm. And if the Holy One, blessed be He, had not brought our fathers forth from Egypt, then surely we, and our children, and our children's children, would be enslaved to Pharaoh in Egypt. And so, even if all of us were full of wisdom and

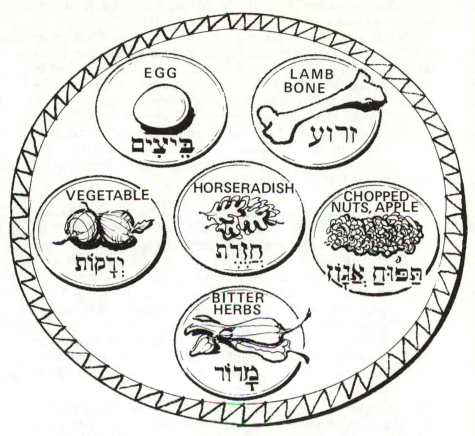

EGG

בֵּיצִים

LAMB BONE

זְרוֹעַ

VEGETABLE

יְרָקוֹת

HORSERADISH

חֲזֶרֶת

CHOPPED NUTS, APPLE

תַּפּוּחַ אֱגוֹז

BITTER HERBS

מָרוֹר

A SEDER PLATE

understanding, well along in years and deeply versed in the tradition, we should still be bidden to repeat once more the story of the exodus from Egypt; and he who delights to dwell on the liberation is a man to be praised.

Through the natural eye, one sees ordinary folk, not much different from their neighbors in dress, language, or aspirations. The words they speak do not describe everyday, commonplace reality and are not meant to. When Jewish people say of themselves, "We were the slaves of Pharaoh in Egypt," they know they themselves felt the lash only through their faith. But it is *their* liberation, not merely that of long-dead forebears, which they now celebrate.

To be a Jew means to be a slave who has been liberated by God. To be "Israel" means to give eternal thanks for God's deliverance. And that deliverance is not at a single moment in historical time. It comes in every generation, is always celebrated. Here again, events of natural, ordinary life are transformed into paradigmatic, eternal, and ever-recurrent sacred moments. Jews think of themselves as having gone forth from Egypt, and Scripture so instructs them. God did not redeem the dead generation of the Exodus alone, but the living too — especially the living. Thus the family states:

> Again and again, in double and redoubled measure, are we beholden to God the All-Present: that He freed us from the Egyptians and wrought His judgment on them; that He sentenced all their idols and slaughtered all their first-born; that He gave their treasure to us and split the Red Sea for us; that He led us through it dry-shod and drowned the tyrants in it; that He helped us through the desert and fed us with the manna; that He gave the Sabbath to us and brought us to Mount Sinai; that He gave the Torah to us and brought us to our homeland — there to build the Temple for us, for atonement of our sins.

> This is the promise which has stood by our forefathers and stands by us. For neither once, nor twice, nor three times was our destruction planned; in every generation they rise against us, and in every generation God delivers us from their hands into freedom, out of anguish into joy, out of mourning into festivity, out of darkness into light, out of bondage into redemption.

> For ever after, in every generation, *every man must think of himself as having gone forth from Egypt* [italics mine]. For we read in the Torah: "In that day thou shalt teach thy son, saying: All this is because of what God did for me when I went forth from Egypt." It was not only our forefathers that the Holy One, blessed be He, redeemed; us too, the living, He redeemed together with them, as we learn from the verse in the Torah: "And He brought us out from thence, so that He might

bring us home, and give us the land which he pledged to our forefathers."

Israel was born in historical time. Historians, biblical scholars, and archaeologists have much to say about that event. But to the Rabbinic Jew, their findings, while interesting, have little bearing on the meaning of reality. The redemptive promise that stood by the forefathers and *stands by the Jew today* is not a mundane historical event, but an interpretation in religious terms of historical, natural events. Oppression, homelessness, extermination, like salvation, homecoming, renaissance — these are this-worldly and profane, supplying headlines for newspapers. The myth that a Jew must think of himself or herself as having gone forth from Egypt, or as we shall see, from Auschwitz, and as being redeemed by God, renders ordinary experience into a moment of celebration. If "we, too, the living, have been redeemed," then the observer no longer witnesses historical human beings in historical time, but an eternal return to a timeless, ever-present mode of being.

The "going forth" to Passover is one sort of exodus. Another comes morning and night when Jews complete their service of worship. Every synagogue service concludes with a prayer prior to going forth, called *Alenu*, from its first word in Hebrew. Like the Exodus, the moment of the congregation's departure becomes a celebration of Israel's God, a self-conscious, articulated rehearsal of Israel's peoplehood. But now it is the end, rather than the beginning, of time that is important. When Jews go forth, they look forward. We read this prayer in connection with the belief in God as ruler of the world. Let us see it again, from another perspective, now as a statement of the self-understanding of the Rabbinic Judaic community.

> Let us praise Him, Lord over all the word;
> Let us acclaim Him, Author of all creation.
> He made our lot unlike that of other peoples;
> He assigned to us a unique destiny.
> We bend the knee, worship, and acknowledge
> the King of kings, the Holy One, praised is He.
> He unrolled the heavens and established the earth;
> His throne of glory is in the heavens above;

His majestic Presence is in the loftiest heights.
He and no other is God and faithful King.
Even as we are told in His Torah:
Remember now and always, that the Lord is God;
Remember, no other is Lord of heaven and earth.
We, therefore, hope in You, O Lord our God,
That we shall soon see the triumph of Your might,
That idolatry shall be removed from the earth,
And false gods shall be utterly destroyed.
Then will the world be a true kingdom of God,
When all mankind will invoke Your name,
And all the earth's wicked will return to You.
Then all the inhabitants of the world will surely know
That to You every knee must bend,
Every tongue must pledge loyalty.
Before You, O Lord, let them bow in worship,
Let them give honor to Your glory.
May they all accept the rule of Your kingdom,
May you reign over them soon through all time.
Sovereignty is Yours in glory, now and forever.
So it is written in Your Torah:
The Lord shall reign for ever and ever.

In secular terms, Jews know that in some ways they form a separate, distinct group. In the religious reality shaped by Rabbinic Judaism, they thank God they enjoy a unique destiny. They do not conclude with thanks for their particular "being," but sing a hymn of hope that he who made their lot unlike that of all others will soon rule as sovereign over all. The secular difference, the unique destiny, is for the time being only. When the destiny is fulfilled, there will be no further difference. The natural eye beholds a social group, with some particular cultural characteristics defining that group. The myth of peoplehood transforms *difference* into *destiny*.

The existence of the natural group means little, except as testimony to the sovereignty of the God who shaped the group and rules its life. The unique, the particular, the private — these now are no longer profane matters of culture, but become testimonies of divine sovereignty, pertinent to all people, all groups. The particularism of the group is for the moment alone; the will of God is for eternity. When that will is done, then all will recognize that the unique destiny of Israel was intended for everyone. The ordinary facts of sociology no longer predominate. The concept of Israel has changed the secular and commonplace into a paradigm of true being.

And what of Israel's long and pathetic history? Is it merely a succession of meaningless disasters, worldly happenings without end or purpose? The answer comes in a folk song sung at the Passover *seder*, the ceremonial meal commemorating the Exodus from Egypt:

> An only kid, an only kid
> My father bought for two pennies,
> An only kid, an only kid.
> But along came the cat and ate up the kid
> My father bought for two pennies.
> An only kid, an only kid.

And so goes the dreary story. Here is the final verse:

> Then the Holy One, blessed be He, came along
> And slew the angel of death
> Who slew the slaughterer
> Who slew the ox
> Who drank the water
> That put out the fire
> That burned the stick
> That beat the dog
> That bit the cat
> That ate the kid
> My father bought for two pennies,
> An only kid, an only kid.

Here is the whole of Israel's history, embodied in an only kid, which the Father bought for next to nothing. The fate of Israel, the lamb slaughtered not once but many times over, is suffering that has an end and a purpose to be understood in the end of days. Death will die, and all who shared in the lamb's suffering will witness the divine denouement of history. The history of sin, suffering, atonement, reconciliation, sin, suffering, atonement, reconciliation — this cycle is not destined forever to repeat itself.

Yet in the worst hour, when all hope is lost, the memories of ancient days, of redemption in olden times, serve to remind Israel of God's enduring concern, of divine pathos. For not once, but many times in the thousands of years of Israel's history, it appeared that the final chapter at last was to be inscribed, and inscribed in blood, on the pages of history. Ezekiel's vision of the dry bones (chapter 37), elevated and exalted in contrast to the humble song of the only kid, ever seems addressed not to the days of old, but to the very present hour:

> The hand of the Lord was upon me, and he brought me out by the Spirit of the Lord, and set me down in the midst of the valley; it was full of bones . . . and lo, they were very dry. And he said to me, "Son of man, can these bones live?" And I answered, "O Lord, God, you know."
>
> And again he said to me, "Prophesy to these bones, and say to them, O dry bones, hear the word of the Lord. Thus says the Lord God to these bones, Behold I will cause breath to enter you, and you shall live. And I will lay sinews upon you and will bring flesh upon you and cover you with skin and put breath in you and you shall live, and you shall know that I am the Lord."

Ezekiel did as he was told,

> So I prophesied as he commanded me, and the breath came into them and they lived and stood upon their feet, an exceedingly great host.
>
> Then he said to me, "Son of man, these bones are the whole house of Israel. Behold, they say, 'Our bones are dried up, and our hope is lost, we are clean cut off.' Therefore prophesy and say to them, Thus says the Lord God, Behold, I will open your graves . . . O my people, and I will bring you home into the land of Israel. And you shall know that I am the Lord, and when I open your graves . . . and I will put my Spirit within you, and you shall live . . . then you shall know that I, the Lord, have spoken and I have done it, says the Lord."

As elsewhere, so here we read words that seem to be addressed uniquely to each generation in its own time and place. What is remarkable about the Judaic tradition is the capacity of diverse historical events to produce recurring and consistent responses, indeed to evoke a single response from varied and unrelated people in all sorts of places. Ezekiel spoke twenty-five centuries ago. His sad words, "Our hope is lost," provide the theme of the national anthem of the State of Israel, "The Hope":

> . . . our hope is not yet lost,
> the hope of two thousand years
> to be a free people in our land
> in the land of Zion and Jerusalem.

What unites the discrete and unrelated events in the life of the "only kid" is the pervasive conviction that an end is coming. Nothing is meaningless, for the random happenings of the centuries are leading to the Messiah. The Messianic hope permeates and illuminates the life of Israel.

Hope for the ideal king of the Messianic age, the *mashiah*, or anointed one (in Greek: Christos), first occurs in biblical times. The first detailed picture of the future ideal king comes in Isaiah 9:1-6, 11:1-10, and 32:1-5. Jeremiah and Ezekiel likewise look forward to the perfect dominion of God's anointed. The Messiah will be of the house of David. The spirit of God will rest on him. He will not conquer nations, but inaugurate a time of peace. He will bring peace, order, and prosperity. Nature will be perfected, so the lamb will not fear the wolf, and society will be made whole, so tyranny and violence will end. Ezekiel emphasizes that in the time of the Messiah, the kingdom of Israel will be restored and reunited. Second Isaiah (ca. 550 B.C.E.) sees Israel, the people, in the messianic role. Israel is the servant of God who will achieve the regeneration of mankind through suffering and service. In pre-Christian times, the messianic hope took the form of a personal Messiah, a scion of David who would end the rule of pagans over the people of God and inaugurate an age of peace and justice.

After the Second Temple was destroyed, in 70 C.E., the rabbis who led Jewry continued to look forward to an earthly Messiah. The form their expectation took is best seen in the prayers they included for daily recitation in Jewish worship. Let us review these prayers, which we have already read:

> Sound the great shofar to herald man's freedom;
> Raise high the banner to gather all exiles;
> Restore our judges as in days of old;
> Restore our counsellors as in former times;
> Remove from us sorrow and anguish.
> Reign over us alone with loving kindness;
> With justice and mercy sustain our cause.
> Praised are You, O Lord, King who loves justice.

The restoration of the exiles to Zion and the gathering of the dispersed are followed naturally by the prayer for good government, government under God's law. Then comes the concrete reference to the Messiah himself:

> Have mercy, O Lord, and return to Jerusalem, Your city;
> May Your presence dwell there as You promised.
> Rebuild it now, in our days and for all time;
> Re-establish there the majesty of David, Your servant.
> Praised are You, O Lord, who rebuilds Jerusalem.
> Bring to flower the shoot of Your servant David.
> Hasten the advent of the Messianic redemption;
> Each and every day we hope for Your deliverance.
> Praised are You, O Lord, who assures our deliverance.

As we have repeatedly seen, the messianic hope thus is inextricably bound with the restoration of the people, the city, the Temple cult, and the house of David.

The history of Israel, the Jewish people, is the history of the only kid; at the end, the Holy One, blessed be He, comes to slaughter the angel of death, vindicate the long sufferings of many centuries, and bring to a happy and joyful end the times of trouble. The messianic hope, made concrete in the figure of the Messiah, son of David and king of Israel, dominates among the elements of the mythic structure of classical Judaism.

Israel's history did not end with the the entry into the land of Canaan, but, rather, began. That history, in a worldly sense, consisted of the secular affairs of a seldom important kingdom, able to hold its own only when its neighbors permitted. In mythic context, however, Jews looked back upon the history of the people as a continuing revelation of divine justice and mercy. Israel kept the Torah; therefore, they enjoyed peace and prospered. Then Israel sinned, so God called forth instruments of his wrath, the Philistines, Assyrians, Babylonians, Persians, Greeks, Romans — there was no end to the list, as time went on. But when Israel was properly chastised, God restored their prosperity and brought them back to the land.

Perhaps the single most powerful worldly experience in the history of Judaism was the destruction of the First Temple, in 586 B.C.E., followed by the restoration of Jews to their land by the Persians, approximately a half-century later. The worldly motives of the Persians are of no interest here, for they never played a role in the interpretation of historical events put forward by Judaic tradition. What the Jews understood was simply this: God had punished them, but when they repented and atoned, he had forgiven and redeemed them. And they further believed that the prophets who had foretold just this pattern of events were now vindicated, so that much else that they had said was likely to be true. From the fifth century B.C.E. to the present, Jews have seen their history within the paradigm of sin, punishment, atonement, reconciliation, then restoration.

The land entered the Judaic imagination as a powerful, indeed overwhelming, symbol. It was holy, the stage for sacred history. We have already noted numerous references to the land, Jerusalem, Zion, and the like. These references all represent concrete exemplifications of myth. Redemption is not an abstract concept, rather it is what happened when Moses led the people through the Sea of Reeds, or what happened with the return to Zion when the Second Temple was built (ca. 500 B.C.E.), or what will happen when God again shines light on Zion and brings the scattered people back to their homes. In Rabbinic Judaism, the sanctity of the land, the yearning for Zion, the hope for the restoration of Jerusalem and the Temple cult — all these are the symbols by which the redemption of the past is projected onto the future. The equivalent of the salvation at the sea will be the restoration of Israel to the land, the reconstruction of the Temple and of Jerusalem: the one stands at the beginning of Israel's history; the other, its counterpart, at the end.

How do the several salvific symbols fit together in the larger structure of creation, revelation, and redemption? In the Grace after Meals, recited whenever pious Jews eat bread, we see their interplay. To understand the setting, one must recall that in Rabbinic Judaism, the table at which meals were eaten was regarded as the equivalent of the sacred alter in the Temple. Pharisaism had taught that each Jew before eating had to attain the same state of ritual purity as the priest in the sacred act of making a sacrifice. So in the classic tradition, the Grace after Meals is recited in a sacerdotal circumstance.

Jews first sing Psalm 126, "When the Lord brought back those that returned to Zion, we were like dreamers. Our mouth was filled with laughter, our tongue with singing. Restore our fortunes, O Lord, as the streams in the dry land. They that sow in tears shall reap in joy . . . ." Then they recite the grace:

> Blessed art Thou, Lord our God, King of the Universe, who nourishes all the world by His goodness, in grace, in mercy, and in compassion: He gives bread to all flesh, for His mercy is everlasting. And because of His great goodness we have never lacked, and so may we never lack, sustenance — for the sake of His great Name. For life nourishes and feeds everyone, is good to all, and provides food for each one of the creatures He created.
>
> Blessed art Thou, O Lord, who feeds everyone.
>
> We thank Thee, Lord our God, for having given our fathers as a heritage a pleasant, a good and spacious land; for having taken us out of the land of Egypt, for having redeemed us from the house of bondage; for Thy covenant, which Thou hast set as a seal in our flesh, for Thy Torah which Thou hast taught us, for Thy statutes which Thou hast made known to us, for the life of grace and mercy Thou has graciously bestowed upon us, and for the nourishment with which Thou dost nourish us and feed us always, every day, in every season, and every hour. For all these things, Lord our God, we thank and praise Thee; may Thy praises continually be in the mouth of every living thing, as it is written. And thou shalt eat and be satisfied, and bless the Lord thy God for the good land which He hath given thee.
>
> Blessed art Thou, O Lord, for the land and its food.

O Lord our God, have pity on Thy people Israel, on Thy city Jerusalem, on Zion the place of Thy glory, on the royal house of David Thy Messiah, and on the great and holy house which is called by Thy Name. Our God, our Father, feed us and speed us, nourish us and make us flourish; unstintingly, O Lord our God, speedily free us from all distress.

And let us not, O Lord our God, find ourselves in need of gifts from flesh and blood, or of a loan from anyone save from Thy full, generous, abundant, wide-open hand; so we may never be humiliated, or put to shame.

O rebuild Jerusalem, the holy city, speedily in our day. Blessed art Thou, Lord, who in mercy will rebuild Jerusalem. Amen.

Blessed art Thou, Lord our God, King of the Universe, Thou God, who art our Father, our powerful King, our creator and redeemer, who made us, our holy one, the holy one of Jacob, our shepherd, shepherd of Israel, the good king, who visits His goodness upon all; for every single day He has brought good, He does bring good, He will bring good upon us; He has rewarded us, does reward, and will always reward us, with grace, mercy and compassion, amplitude, deliverance and prosperity, blessing and salvation, comfort, and a living, sustenance, pity and peace, and all good — let us not want any manner of good whatever!

The context of grace is enjoyment of creation, through which God nourishes the world in his goodness. That we have had this meal — however humble — is not to be taken for granted. Whenever one eats, he or she must reflect on the beneficence of the creator. The arena for creation is the land, which to the ordinary eye is commonplace, small, dry, rocky, but to the eye of faith is pleasant, good, spacious. The land lay at the end of redemption from Egyptian bondage. Holding it, enjoying it — as we saw in the *Shema* — is a sign that the covenant is intact and in force, and that Israel is loyal to its part of the contract, God to his. The land, the Exodus, the covenant — these all depend upon the Torah, statutes, a life of grace and mercy, here embodied in and evoked by, the nourishment of the meal. Thanksgiving wells up, and the verse ends with praises for the land and its food.

Then the chief theme recurs, redemption and hope for return, and finally future prosperity in the land: "May God pity the people, the city, Zion, the royal house of the Messiah, the holy Temple." The nourishment of this meal is but a foretaste of the nourishment of the messianic time, just as the joy of the wedding is a foretaste of the messianic rejoicing.

Still, it is not the messianic time, so Israel finally asks not to depend upon the gifts of mortals, but only upon those of the generous, wide-open hand of God. And then "rebuild Jerusalem." The conclusion summarizes the whole, giving thanks for creation, redemption, divine goodness, every blessing.

In some liturgies, creation takes the primary place, as here and in the wedding ceremony. In others, the chief theme is revelation. Redemptive symbols occur everywhere.

Timelessness and Eternity

By this point in your examination of the authoritative prayers of Rabbinic Judaism, you may have wondered about my assertion in the opening chapter of this book. There I claimed that Rabbinic Judaism took shape around the ideal of timelessness, against the widely held conviction that the Messiah was even then about to come. I further posed as separate and distinct alternatives the ideal of Messianism, with its concern for the meaning of events, and the ideal of Rabbinic Judaism, with its concern for continuities. Messianism means that we pay very close attention to the meaning of great events and seek to understand where we are going, and when we shall get there. Rabbinic Judaism, by contrast, proposes to create a timeless world, a metahistorical community, capable of riding out the waves of history and the vicissitudes of time by creating a life of eternity and unchanging sanctity in the here and now.

Yet when you go back over the prayers we have read, you see in virtually every single one a reference to redemption, to the coming of the Messiah, to the messianic images of the Land of Israel, Zion, and Jerusalem. And these are, most assuredly, prayers taught by Rabbinic Judaism, recited by Jews who believe firmly and completely in the two Torahs — the one whole Torah — of that mode of Judaism.

Surely I seem to be wrong, therefore, in my original assertion. The great alternative to the Messianism, the concentration on the meaning and end of history, is nothing more than another kind of Messianism.

I believe that is, in fact, correct — but with a difference. And the difference is important. True, the rabbinic Messianism laid forth in the liturgy does stress redemption, as we have observed. But it is a redemption dependent upon Torah, on the one side, and God's will, on the other. Rabbinic Messianism places a limit upon the "timeless reality" created by the rabbinic Torah. It never intended to posit an endless mode of being, absolutely above history. Rabbinic Judaism, quite to the contrary, proposes to remove the messianic question from the everyday and the here and now, to place it where it belongs, at the end of time and in the hand of God.

What the rabbis created was a way of living *as if* and *until* — until the Messiah will come. The nonhistorical, nontimebound quality of the rabbinic mode of life and thought is for the present, that continuing, timeless present which stretches from Sinai to the coming of the King Messiah. Then, but *only* then, the timeless present ends. It ends, it is clear, at eternity.

So the timeless mode of being, forever in the here and now, is a foretaste of the messianic time — *as if* the Messiah were here — and the purpose of Rabbinic Judaism, in a curious and paradoxical way, must be seen as the effort to realize as much of eternity as mortal men and women can accomplish in an unredeemed world.

In other words, the rabbis took seriously the condition of humankind, its unredemption and imperfection, and proposed as the remedy to that condition a grand messianic experiment. They would reach out toward the messianic age by the improvement of the human condition in accord with the teaching of the Torah — the whole Torah of Moses, "our rabbi." The rabbis' conviction was and is that the Messiah will come "when all Israel keeps a single Sabbath," or, to put it more generally, when all Israel becomes the kingdom of priests and the holy people that the Torah was meant to create.

What the rabbis have done, therefore, is to impose the matter of Torah upon the issue of redemption, just as they

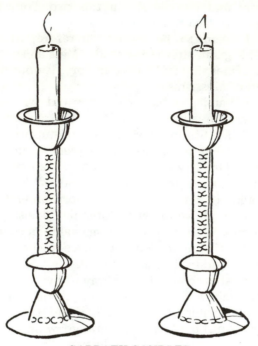

SABBATH CANDLES

place Torah's stamp upon the conception of revelation and of creation, as we say in the *Shema*. The issue was phrased provocatively, but perhaps too sharply, in the opening chapter: *Messiah versus timeless Torah*. The redemptive plan of Rabbinic Judaism is best expressed as *Messiah by means of Torah*.

Yet even if that is self-evidently the case, still we have to take seriously the rabbinic life-beyond-history, Rabbinic Judaism's ultimate indifference to the events of the here and now. For the stress of Rabbinic Judaism clearly is on the humble continuities of home and hearth, society and the streets, rather than upon the elevated issues of politics, nations, and other truly historical concerns. Messiah yes — but at the end of time. And, as I just said, at the end of the timeless and unchanging rabbinic way of life lies not more history, but redemption and eternity, even now realized in Torah.

When we discover what happened to Judaism in modern times, the one important, striking trait is going to be the renewed interest, on the part of some Jews, in the meaning and importance of the historical here and now, the real, this-worldly condition of the Jewish people, and the consequent renewal of the messianic activity so characteristic of the first century C.E. What makes modern Jews modern, in other words, is going to be — in the first instance at least — their vivid messianic hope and the consequent messianic movements they created.

Now that the central issue of Rabbinic Judaism, the human concern to which the religion of Torah is addressed, is clear in our minds, we should be ready to approach the modern age. Yet, before we take our leave of the timeless world of Torah, we should ask, What are the simple, human virtues yielded by Torah? How did a person live his or her life under its effect? What were the primary personal goals that an individual sought to attain? To answer this question, we allude, in conclusion, to a charming literature generated by Rabbinic Judaism, the literature of ethical wills. People would write wills in which they distributed not their worldly wealth but their slender treasury of wisdom and piety. One such legacy is that of Joel, son of Abraham Shemariah, who died in 1799.

To his children, he wrote, "To be at peace with all the world, with Jew and Gentile, must be your foremost aim in this

A SPICE BOX FOR HAVDALAH

earthly life. Contend with no one. In the first instance your home must be the abode of quietude and happiness. No harsh word must be heard there, but over all must reign love, amity, modesty, and a spirit of gentleness and reverence. This spirit must not end with the home, however. In your dealings with the world you must allow neither money nor ambition to disturb you. Forego your rights, envy no one. For the main thing is peace, peace with the whole world. Show all men every possible respect, deal with them in the finest integrity and faithfulness. For Habakkuk [2:4] summed up the whole Torah in the one sentence, 'The righteous shall live by his faith.' "[2]

That, it is clear, is the natural outcome of a religion that aimed at overcoming the vicissitudes of history and at finding a safe harbor, an eternal refuge, against the storms of time.

Notes

1. Discussion on how the Mishnah works appeared in *Keeping Posted*, Vol. XX, No. 4, January, 1975, under the title, "Putting Holiness into Words: The Mishnah and Its Laws," © 1975 by the Union of American Hebrew Congregations. It is reprinted here by permission.

2. Israel Abrahams, ed., *Hebrew Ethical Wills* (Philadelphia: Jewish Publication Society of America), 1948, II, pp. 344-5.

Chapter Three
Judaism in Modern Times: New Messianism, Renewed Torah

The New Age

In modern times the Jews, along with the rest of human-kind, underwent changes so important that the entire social and economic basis of their lives was altered, and the foundations of Judaic religious expression were radically revised. Our concern is for the history of Judaism, but the history of Judaism and the history of the Jews cannot be distinguished from one another. The history of Judaism forms the mind and imagination of the Jews. And the history of the Jews supplies the raw materials for interpretation and understanding which all together add up to Judaism.

What is the dominant trait of the modern world? It is change made permanent, persistent revolution. Karl Marx observed in 1847, "The bourgeoisie during its rule of scarcely one hundred years has created more massive and more colossal productive forces than have all the preceding generations put together." Formerly society in which the Jews lived was based upon a fixed status, upon authority structured in a hierarchy, upon guilds and corporations, upon local autonomy, and upon historic peculiarity. In that society Jews had a recognized place. But, beginning in the nineteenth century, society was based upon social mobility, and careers were open to talent and

115

individual initiative. Traditional communities such as had been formed by the Jews were formerly held together by unquestioned religious faith. Now they were broken up into parties and classes.

Above all we witness the rise of individualism, according to the individual all rights and the power to decide one's destiny. Individualism involved a demand for happiness, a faith in the power of technology and in the capacity of humankind to solve its problems. Now all traditional beliefs were called into question. Universal and abstract patterns of relationship were substituted for local, national, and ethnic or racial distinctiveness. There was therefore a vast issue of change affecting everyone, including the Jews. The spiritual moorings, which had held things together for many, many centuries were cut loose. There was a new faith, a faith in history moving in preordained, predetermined ways, so that contradictions of social existence would soon be resolved. In other words, when we come to the nineteenth century, we come to a new age in which men and women had the sense of witnessing and participating in vast changes for the better.

The modern period in the history of Judaism is marked by the striking phenomenon of the continuation of the way of living and believing which we have been studying to this point. We cannot overlook not only the persistence, but the flourishing, of classical, traditional Judaism — the way of Torah — up to the present day. Now, in the last third of the twentieth century, many Jews throughout the world, including nearly all religious Jews in the state of Israel, stand in an unbroken connection to that form of Judaism called Rabbinic. Many Jews live their lives entirely in conformity to classical Judaism, its laws and doctrine, and these people continue the rabbinic tradition. Furthermore, Reform, Conservative, and Modern or Western Orthodox Jews link up with that rabbinic tradition. The traditionalist group as well as its modern derivatives do not stand merely as fossils or relics. They transmit a mode of living and a way of interpreting Jewish existence, and also enrich that mode of life.

Until the middle of the twentieth century, in fact, most Jews in Eastern Europe and large numbers in Central Europe remained Orthodox; large parts of Western Jewry likewise formed wholly observant communities which maintained the rabbinic way of living and understanding the world. The movements upon which we shall lay our stress affected only small parts of the entire Jewish people in the nineteenth century. It is a serious error to understand these movements as telling the whole story. The problems and the changes before us affected these same Jews of the East as they did the communities of the West. Traditional society produced its response, which was entirely authentic to the old rabbinic way, within the modes of expression and values that we have already studied. All modes of Judaism in the modern world, by definition, are modern. They share a common context of problems and change, responding to the conditions of modern life, and taking into account the same reality, but each in its own way.

Let us first consider the two events in the modern history of the Jews that most decisively shaped the modern history of Judaism: Emancipation and anti-Semitism.

Political "Emancipation" is the extension to Jews of the rights and privileges of full citizenship in the various countries in which they lived. The first country to grant it was the United States. Its Constitution extended full and equal rights to all Americans. Of greater immediate consequence was the Emancipation of French Jewry in the aftermath of the Revolution of 1789. Later, in the nineteenth century, British, German, and other Western European Jews achieved the same rights.

What in fact had changed? Medieval society was organized by estates into a corporate society. Each estate had a specific status in law and life. As we have seen, that fact conformed to the realities of Jewish life. Jews had no reason to reject recognition as a particular class or estate among other such "corporations." If Jews were later given "equality," they thereby lost their ethnic-religious autonomy. The modern state demanded the abolition of corporate distinctions, seeking to make all men equal under the law, and equally obligated to serve the state. Emancipation in the form of the provision of equal rights, therefore, was a mixed blessing, especially so because of the universal failure fully to realize those rights and to construct a society of equal opportunity and responsibility. This meant that Jewry had lost in security and autonomy more than it had gained in liberty and freedom. Traditional religious values were undermined; new values and ideals, which took their place, tended to separate Jews from the classical tradition, but to provide them with no certain ideals at all. Jews indeed were expected to "assimilate," that is, to cease being Jews at all, as condition of their "acceptance" by Gentiles. It is clear that Emancipation posed the most serious challenge to the Jews, as well as to their religious tradition, since the destruction of the First Temple in 586 B.C.E.

The crisis brought on by the shaking of the sociological foundations of Judaism was greatly intensified by growing anti-Semitism in Western countries, culminating in what Jews universally call "the Holocaust." By this they refer to the destruction of approximately six million European Jews between 1933 and 1945. This historical event dominates Judaic theology today, just as it shapes the imagination of the Jewish people in many lands. To understand why, one must realize the difference between the Holocaust and all former massacres, riots, expulsions, and other calamities suffered by Jewry over millennia. The first difference is quantitative; six million Jews represented one out of every three Jews in the world in 1939. In all of human history, only the massacre of two million of the four million Armenian people by the Turks and Germans in World War I is comparable. And of all Jews alive in lands conquered by Germany after 1939, nearly 90 percent died.

The second difference was the racist character of the Holocaust. When Christians killed Jews, they would spare those who converted to Christianity; but the Nazis spared no one, regarding as a Jew someone who had only a single Jewish grandparent. Formerly, Jews might be expelled. Now, no one was permitted to escape. As Raul Hilberg puts it, "The missionaries of Christianity had said in effect, You have no right to live among us as Jews. The secular rulers who followed had proclaimed, You have no right to live among us. The German Nazis at last decreed, You have no right to live."

The third, and single most important difference was that the Holocaust was the achievement of an efficient, modern industrial state, prepared to invest vast efforts and sums in the creation of an industry producing one thing only: dead Jews. Nothing episodic, sporadic, or occasional characterized the Holocaust. On the contrary, it was systematic, orderly, well planned, superbly carried out. Despite the need for war transport for troops, train schedules were drawn up to move hundreds of thousands, eventually millions, of human beings;

despite the scarcity of men and material, great concentration camps were built and staffed; gas chambers were manufactured even in preference to war production; corpses were carefully devoted to useful ends, such as the manufacture of soap. True, Nazi special forces would also gather together Jewish communities in front of large ditches, then machine-gun the whole lot; but these special actions, carried out mainly in newly conquered territories in the east, could not in a few years have accounted for millions of people. The great bureaucracy required for this task, operating with accelerating speed and ever-widening destructive effect, proceeded to annihilate the European Jews.

To understand the impact of the Holocaust on the contemporary Jewish mind, one need only to imagine himself a Jew and to live with the knowledge and the nightmare that had he been in Europe, he would have died on that account. There was no way out. The nations of the world did practically nothing after 1939, little enough before then. Nor did salvation come from another place.

Modern Judaism was the creation of European Jewry. And European Jewry was moving inexorably to destruction. Its creations lived on, in various ways, in America, Britain, Israel, and elsewhere, so that there is hardly an idea or an institution of contemporary Jewry whose roots do not go deep into nineteenth century Europe. The historical foundation of modern Judaism, is, therefore, deeply flawed. Raul Hilberg writes: "Jewry is faced with ultimate weapons. It has no deterrent. The Jews can live more freely now. They can also die more quickly. The summit is within sight. An abyss has opened below." If what happened to the ancient Israelites bore heavy implications for the shape of Israelite religion, the same is so today. If the Exodus led to Sinai, then where does Auschwitz lead? What are its religious implications? One who broods on that perplexity has encountered the contemporary Jewish situation.

The End of Traditional Society

Jacob Katz, an Israeli historian, provides a comprehensive account of "traditional Judaism" on the threshold of modernization. Defining "traditional society" as "a type of society which regards its existence as based upon a common body of knowledge and values handed down from the past," Katz stresses the commonalities of religion, nationhood, and messianic hope, and traces the disintegrative effect upon them of religious charisma in Hasidism, and of rationalism in the Jewish Enlightenment.

To the end of the eighteenth century, when the "modern period" of the history of Judaism begins, Jewish society was corporate, segregated, and collective in emphasis. Jews in Europe spoke a common language, Yiddish, and regarded themselves as a separate nation, living within other nations and awaiting their ultimate return to their own land. The central social ideal was study of Torah, which would result in heavenly reward. The obligation to study the Torah, leading to an intense appreciation for intellectualism, prevented the sanctification of economic activity as an ultimate goal, and insured effective control over the people's value structure. Study of tradition was the chief purpose of living. The community itself was governed by its own classical legal tradition, with the rabbi as judge and community official.

The *kehillah*, or "structure of community government" controlled economic activities, relations with non-Jews, family and social life, and matters of religion, including, of course, all aspects of culture and education. It was the structural embodiment of the corporate community.

How did this community disintegrate, so that the focus of Judaism came to center upon the individual, and the emphasis of Jewish thought, upon the individual's personal religious needs and convictions? It was not the result of external catastrophes. Jewish society was badly shaken by massacres in 1648-49, but the response of the community, as Katz points out, did not deviate from the traditional pattern: "There is no record of any program of action being instituted to prevent the recurrence of such an event . . . no political or social conclusions were drawn from the historical experience. As a matter of fact, the realistic explanations were overshadowed by the traditional view of divine providence, so that the lesson that emerged from the stocktaking was a religious-moral one." It took the form of fasting, prayer, severe sumptuary laws, and rededication to study and observance of the Torah.

During the eighteenth century it was Hasidism in Eastern

Europe, and *Haskalah*, or "Enlightenment," in the West, that undermined traditional society. These movements shattered the framework of the community which had formerly been able to reconstitute itself following banishments and migrations.

Hasidism, a pietist movement recalling the contemporary Methodism of Britain and the Great Awakening of mid-eighteenth-century New England, weakened the fidelity of the people to the rabbinic lawyer's leadership by stressing the importance *not* of learning the law, but of religious charisma, the capacity to say particularly effective prayers, tell evocative stories, and work wonders. Existing institutions seem to have lost their hold on large numbers of people. The situation was ripe for new social groups to take shape among people who had lost faith in the old ones. The Hasidic rabbi, called *Tzaddik* (literally, "righteous one"), won the loyalty of such people through the force of his personality. He was regarded not as a mere wonder-worker, but as an intermediary between heaven and earth.

Hasidism was more than an adjustment to new social conditions or a movement of protest. In content, value, and structure, it was a revolution that set in a new light all preceding faith. One achieved holiness through Torah, or through the *Tzaddik* and celebrating his holiness, but not through both. A movement within the community, Hasidism created sects in the traditional corporate society. Some followed the charismatic leaders; others did not. The consequence of these doctrines and policies was a religious and social revolution based upon a new requirement for leadership: not learning but personality. It resulted in the formation, within the body of the old community, of new and limited societies; in consequence, the traditional *kehillah* was destroyed.

The second force for modernization of traditional society was the Enlightenment in France and Germany, which altogether revolutionized the basis of Jewish society by destroying both its legal and its philosophical foundation. External rather than internal in its impact, the Enlightenment withdrew the political basis of Jewry by extending to Jews the rights of citizens, and at the same time denying Judaism the authority over Jews it had formerly exercised. It furthermore encouraged the development within Jewry of a new type of person, the *maskil*, "illumined man," who mastered areas of human erudition formerly thought to be irrelevant to Jews. So the Enlightenment's processes of dissolution reinforced one another. The *kehillah* lost its legal standing, and some of its subjects opted out of it at the same time.

Now individual members of Jewish society began to interest themselves in the opinion of the Gentile world and to seek the esteem of non-Jews on the basis of Gentile values. Had Jews merely converted to Christianity, it would hardly have affected traditional society; but many left that society and yet chose to remain Jews. They plunged into a crisis of identity which has yet to find resolution.

As part of the Jewish community — though perhaps on its fringes — the *maskilim* held up to the tests of reason, intelligence, and nature the artifacts of the tradition that had formerly been accepted as part of the given, or the revealed reality, of the world. And they did so aggressively and derisively. The values they projected were those of the neutral society, which they saw as the "wave of the future." They criticized the economic structure of Jewish society, its occupational one-sidedness, the traditional organizations whose compulsory authority they rejected, and the traditional system of education which did nothing to prepare young people to participate in the new world then seen to be opening up.

They did not propose to abandon Jewish society, but to "modernize" it. Values formerly held to be ends in themselves now came to be evaluated in terms of their usefulness and rationality, a usefulness measured not within the Jewish framework at all. The synagogue was seen as the assembly of the faithful for prayer, rather than as the focus for community life, society, and culture, as in former times. The content and language of prayer, the architecture of the synagogue and its ritual — all these were among the earliest objects of a reformation. Most significantly, the traditional modes of social control — denunciation, excommunication — ceased to operate effectively. The "deviant" no longer saw himself as a sinner. He did not justify himself by traditional values at all.

Modernization was hardly a broad, widespread phenomenon. It mattered in only a very few places, and even there unevenly, to almost the present time. Though the *kehillah* in its late medieval form underwent vast changes, the traditional personality and living pattern of Jews in many lands did not.

The Enlightenment's impact, even in Germany until well into the nineteenth century, was limited to the upper classes. Hasidism was a mostly regional phenomenon, and after two generations, its fervor was directed into more or less traditional channels. Today, while remaining highly sectarian, it has become a bastion of "the tradition" in its least malleable form.

More broadly still, the Jews in Muslim countries, apart from the Gallicized urban upper classes, remained deeply a part of the traditional culture, not so much affirming intellectual reasons for remaining so, as practicing the faith in its classical forms, into the twentieth century. For many, arriving in the State of Israel also signified arrival in the twentieth century as we know it. The political changes we associated under the title of emancipation never reached Polish, Rumanian, and Russian Jewry — the vast majority of the Jewish people — before the Holocaust of 1933 to 1945. Furthermore, for many Jews in Western countries, the experience of modernization was objectionable; and, as we shall see, many rejected it. If a tradition changes, it is only for some; it never disintegrates for all.

It would be impossible to offer a fully adequate delimitation of the modernization of Judaism for three reasons.

First, substantial parts of the Jewish people, including those in Muslim countries and large segments of Eastern European Jewry, never underwent such a process.

Second, even in the great cities, to which the majority of Central and Western European Jews had come by 1900, significant populations of traditionalists existed to the time of the Holocaust, and, in the Western countries, to the present day. Whether they are traditional in the way in which the seventeenth-century Jew was traditional is not the issue. The fact is that those qualities we have associated with traditionalism apply without qualification to large parts of Jewry, and therefore to significant segments of Judaism in Israel, the United States, Great Britain, continental Europe, and elsewhere.

Third, the inner dynamism of a living tradition is such that at no point may we arbitrarily arrest its development for purposes of definition, and conclude that a given form is "*the* tradition" from which all that changes thereby deviates and therefore constitutes "modernization." Within the circles of the most traditional Jews, cultural phenomena are today accepted that a century ago would have been regarded as unacceptable, and yet should we call such Jews "Modernists" the term would be deprived of any meaning whatever. In context they think of themselves, and are thought of by others, as living within the classic tradition.

Thus far we have briefly reviewed important changes in the political and social situation in which Judaism existed. We have seen that tremendous political events redefined the status and role of the Jew in society. He or she was no longer viewed as part of a community, but as autonomous. Major internal events broke up the corporate community, just as the political setting was changing. At the same time, we stress, Rabbinic Judaism, the timeless world created nineteen centuries earlier and rising above change, continued to flourish. We are going to examine two great messianic movements which took seriously the vast changes of the modern world and regarded events as significant and augural.

But let us first take note of how the old way continued in the age which some regarded as utterly new and unprecedented. For the issue before Judaism in modern times was and is whether the "modern" is new and unprecedented, bearing its own innovative meaning, or whether "modern times" simply mark another stage in the ongoing history of humanity, a history to be endured as best one can until the Messiah comes. The contrast between Rabbinic Judaism and modern Messianic Judaisms is simple. The one found itself capable of coping with change. The other insisted change mattered. Whether change is good, as Messianic Reform Judaism in the nineteenth century maintained, or whether change is bad, as Messianic Zionism held, both parties regarded as an important fact what Rabbinic Judaism took in stride. In terms of our original paradigm, the former groups focused upon the meaning of historical events and asked about where they were heading. The latter group persisted in attending to matters of eternity.

Strengthening the Foundations

Two aspects to the response of Rabbinic Judaism to the modern crisis interest us.

The first we treat briefly. It is the view that "the new is prohibited." One significant, continuing, and persistent response thus was the utter negation of modernity, the claim that it is both possible and necessary to reject modernity in every form and to continue, in exactly the old ways, in the classical faith. There was to be no recognition of, and no negotiation or compromise with, modernity.

That such a response was both possible and effective is shown by the large number of Jews throughout the world who do indeed continue to maintain and nurture the classic forms of rabbinic life and thought in much the way in which they have been handed on. It would be foolish to suppose that the persistence of the old patterns is not feasible, that it is inevitable that the old must give way to the new. The contrary already has been demonstrated. The new can be rejected, the old both preserved and enhanced. To regard as "fossils" the modes of Orthodoxy, which reject modernization and Westernization including all artifacts of Western culture and science, is simply to place a negative valuation, based on one's own conception of what is right and necessary, upon what is clearly a vital response to modernity.

The negative response to modernity is best represented by Moses Sofer (1762-1839), who taught, "What is new is prohibited by the Torah," an extreme and carefully thought through position. There was to be no compromise. The "emancipation" of the Jews, that is, the bestowal upon them of the equal rights and social status of all citizens, was not to be welcomed but to be rejected. The appeal of Western culture was to be ignored. It is not as though Moses Sofer did not know what was happening. On the contrary, he examined the situation of Jews in the West, indeed was well aware of the movements of modernized Judaism in Germany. He knew precisely what he did not like. It was not ignorance of the appeal of the West, but rather full awareness of its dangers to something he deemed holy and of abiding truth, that led him to prohibit all that was new.

At the same time, he recognized that one could not simply stand firm and still. If the tradition was to endure, it had to be firmly implanted in peoples' lives, and this meant that new and effective means of education had to be worked out. If Moses Sofer was intransigent in the face of modernity, he was radical in his approach to what was important and had to be made effective, the educational institutions and programs of the community. Within the bastion of the faith, Sofer thought, reform must go forward. Beyond it, Reform must be opposed. It was a consistent policy. The Jews were to be offered the choice of Orthodoxy, in its traditional form, or apostasy. There was to be no middle way.

The second response of classical rabbinism to the modern situation is that of Israel Salanter (1786-1866), who took seriously the aspirations of Western Jewry and attempted to show a better way of reform than Reform. Salanter knew that the human dilemmas of the Western Jews could not be ignored, nor could those Jews be offered an impossible choice, the denial of two things which meant much to them and which came into conflict, the tradition and the new age.

Salanter's stress on ethical behavior was remarkably congruent to the emphasis on acceptable citizenship important to Western Jews, but it rested upon much firmer foundations. To Salanter, ethics was not merely socially expedient, but of sacred importance. It was the center of the religious life, the primary mode of service to God. Salanter's response to the modern condition derived directly, and without mediation, from Rabbinic Judaism's classical emphasis on practical action.

Salanter sought a balance between intellectualism and saintliness. By study of the ethical literature of Rabbinic Judaism he would show a better way. To him this did not mean that one should study only Jewish learning. He understood the importance of mastering secular sciences and skills, though these were of merely contingent importance. He himself lived in Germany and therefore confronted the new age, as other rabbinical authorities of Eastern Europe did not. Like Moses Sofer, he believed the spreading knowledge of the Talmud would cure the ailment of Israel. But he had the vision to recognize that, if the Talmud was good for Israel, it also was good for the Gentiles, for its rationality and dialectic logic would improve the minds of all who devoted themselves to its discipline. It was a visionary notion, but revealing of the man's interest in the changing world and his openness to its opportunities.

What did Salanter seek to establish? Familiar as we now are with some of the high points of earlier Rabbinic Judaism, we may readily propose the answer: to serve, and teach others to serve, God. This means to do the right deed for the right reason, and requires that a person overcome what is natural in the supernatural discipline of the Torah. The goal of learning is not learning, but moral intelligence.

Like the Hasidim of his day, he meditated deeply on the nature and dual character of humankind. Through meditation and exercise of self-control human beings would overcome the impulse to do evil and discipline themselves to do good. Self-search and self-criticism was the way. Salanter aimed at creating a discipline — a habit — to lead to perpetual mindfulness, ingrained alertness to what one did and thought. One should have supposed "mindfulness" and "habit" are opposite of one another. But by finding a *routine* of thoughtfulness, Salanter hoped to transform the habitual into the holy. Virtue must be made "automatic" yet intentional. He held that through asceticism and self-sacrifice one would attain the spiritual goals to which he or she aspired. Louis Ginzberg summarizes the teaching of Salanter as follows:

> The keynote of his teaching is that the aim and task of the Jew is to strive to secure the ethically ideal condition of man and of the world, no matter how far off and perhaps unreachable it may be. Judaism is for him no theoretical system, teaching speculative truths or scientific knowledge concerning a certain province of thought, but it is a doctrine intended to lead man to his moral ennoblement by prescribed ways and means. So far as the moral life is concerned the concrete plays a preponderating and decisive part. On the other hand it cannot dispense with speculative or, let us rather say, religious truths. In fact, it requires some religious truths as a support and a guarantee for the binding force of the moral law. Other religious truths, again, strengthen the will, or are of spiritual value in moral development, because they fuse together practice and theory into a harmonious unity. If morality is to be not merely a theory but a real factor in the life of man, he must so train his thoughts and feelings that his moral consciousness becomes too strong to allow him to act otherwise than morally. The religious truths which are indispensi-

ble to the ethical education of man and without which
he cannot develop morally, are: Belief in God, Revelation, and Reward and Punishment.

We have seen above what important role the doctrine
of Reward and Punishment plays in his teachings, and
we may add here that Revelation or, to use the
rabbinical term, the Torah is of still greater consequence. In his public addresses, Salanter hardly ever
touched on any other subject than ethics and the study
of the Torah. The latter is to be considered from two
different angles. First, as the revealed will of God, it is
the only safe guide for our religious and moral life.
Hence the duty incumbent upon every one, not only on
the professional scholar, to occupy himself with the
study of the Torah that his conduct may always be in
accordance with the divine Will. The study of the Jewish
civil code however, to take one instance, is a religious
work not only because it enables the student to know
what is right and what is wrong in a given case, but also
because it refines and deepens one's conscience. Consequently, strange as it may sound, it is from the point of
view of religion more important for the business man
than for the Rabbi — the judge — to be thoroughly
acquainted with the civil code. The former is often
tempted to dishonesty, and by continuous study of the
commercial law of the Torah he will be in a better
position to withstand his temptations, of which the
Rabbi is innocent. Besides the practical parts of the
Torah, the study of any portion thereof is a remedy
against the Yezer. "The spirit emanating from the Torah
makes spiritual him who occupies himself with it."[1]

We see, therefore, that the modern world produced important
voices speaking the language of Rabbinic Judaism. These voices
should be heard by us because they are listened to, as we have
stressed, by the larger number of Jews who regard themselves as
religious. We notice in the discussion of Salanter's teaching
precisely the images — the appeal to Torah — we should find at
any point in the history of Judaism from the first century
onward.

There is still another very large group of Jews not to be

ignored. These are the Jews who left Judaism entirely and also ceased to regard themselves as belonging to the Jewish community. If we were studying the history of the Jewish people in the nineteenth and twentieth centuries we should have to devote much attention to ex-Jews. But what do we learn of Judaism, whether of the rabbinic type or any other, from people who decisively reject the old form and make no effort at shaping a new one? All we learn — and it is an important fact — is that for many people Judaism became a dead religion, just as for many people born in Christian homes Christianity in any form ceased to present a meaningful alternative. We learn, therefore, that the powerful current of secularization swept over the Jews as it did throughout the West.

Those people who abandoned Judaism and whose children were brought up totally without a consciousness that they belonged to the Jewish group do not form an important topic in the study of Judaism. But there is another vast and important group, the Jews who explored what they conceived to be new paths. These are the ones who remained within the Jewish group, seeking to construct a new definition of the meaning of being Jewish. Among these we have to make still another distinction. We have to see the difference between people who, while remaining Jewish, dropped all connections with a religious understanding of themselves as Jews, and those who sought a mode of religious expression other than the inherited and enduring one embodied in the traditionalism of a Moses Sofer or an Israel Salanter. Both kinds of Jews — nontraditional religious and nontraditional secular — present important testimonies in the study of modern Judaism. They have much in common.

What they have in common we may describe with the word messianic; the two most consequential and influential expressions of modern Judaism are the messianic movements of Reform Judaism and Zionism. Reform Judaism stands for those who preserve the religious approach to life, and Zionism speaks in particular to those who do not. What these two massive movements share is a concentration upon the meaning of great events. Reform Judaism and Zionism take with upmost serious-ness the history of the modern world, each interpreting that history, those events, in its own way, but in common agreeing that the world was changing and moving towards a climax. What distinguishes Rabbinic Judaism in modern times from Messianic Judaism in its two major formulations is the understanding and appreciation of change. Rabbinic Judaism knows full well that from the first century to the twentieth much has happened. What Rabbinic Judaism maintains, however, is this: Amid change and storm Torah endures. The realm of holiness marked off in time by sacred days, marked off in life by devotion to learning in Torah, endures.

Messianic Judaism differs because in its several forms it affirms that Jews live in extraordinary times. Vast opportunities for the permanent and final perfection of the world and of the condition of the Jewish people are present. Taking events seriously, Reform Judaism and Zionism both affirm that the Jewish people have passed through a long dark age and should now come to the rest and solace, to the best and final age in history. Let us now turn to the movements and examine their characteristics.

Reform Judaism

"The old temple of medieval Ghetto Judaism may be in ruins but the new one of Messianic Judaism is taking shape," said Emil G. Hirsch to the American Reform rabbis in 1895. It would be difficult to find a more succinct statement of the conception held by the Reform Judaism of the age and of the task before it. Hirsch spoke of the coming of God's kingdom on earth. It was his hope, shared by the reformers of Judaism, that through the small reform of the Jewish tradition the messianic age would be attained. Let us listen to his message:

> Other religions speak of a paradise lost to be regained somewhere beyond the clouds. Judaism points to a future to be won here, and not by one, by all humanity. It is true, the picture of the future state, as painted by the prophets and cherished by Israel in centuried exile, displays politico-national coloring. Yet even so, it abounds in tints glorifying the triumph of justice universal, simultaneous with national restoration. The latter was only an episode in the great oratorio of

universal redemption. We have learned to forget the national incident personified in the Messianic king, in the grander outlook into the Messianic age of universal justice and worthiness ascendant. It has been well said, Christianity pivots on individual salvation, Judaism hinges on social redemption and regeneration. The *Olam Habba* [world to come] of our religion is not a state *in heaven*. It is God's Kingdom *on earth*. These ethical principles, then, founded on the apprehension of God's unity, i.e., the oneness of the universal purpose running through creation, its essential righteousness, and of God's and man's *at-one-ness*, are the characteristic contribution made by Judaism to man's wealth. They constitute the one pillar of Judaism, while the other is the self-consciousness of the Jew rooted in his sense of responsibility for the illustration and spreading abroad during days of good and bad report, by example, of these ideas original in his historic life. The Jew being in the historic line of descent, the heir of those who first learned to view man and God in such relation, receives by birth the duty to illustrate by his own life and his own conduct that man is divine, that sanctity is not denied him, that justice may be done on earth, to emphasize his belief in the final triumph of righteousness and love and humanity in the Messianic age, God's Kingdom come.

So Judaism is, after all, not a mere religion; it is more than a religion which one may accept or reject.

No Jew has the right to accept or reject Judaism. It is a call, a duty, that comes to him with the accident of birth from a Jewish mother, or let me rather say, it is providential appointment! We cannot choose our parents; we cannot elect our duties. Some would desert; what boot to them? The curse follows them, haunts them. Blood in their case is a stigma which water will not wash. A Reform Jew will never abandon his historic post. He understands that the Jew is called to be the illustrator of prophetic fundamental conceptions and principles which solve the riddle of the universe and also answer the enigmas of the human heart. This Judaism, the radical believes in and would practice. It is this

Judaism of which the radical wants more, not less. The radical realizes that to carry out their mission the Jews shall live lives of righteousness. If from righteousness they depart, they commit blasphemy; they deny God "Hillul Hashem." For it is only by the righteous life illustrating the divinity of man, that this divinity is verified. Judaism is under law — the law of righteousness; but in no other sense is the Jew under the law.

We have to take seriously Hirsch's emphasis on the affirmative aspects of Reform Judaism. He stresses that a Reform Jew will never abandon his historic post. We misunderstand Reform Judaism if we regard it as a road out of the tradition. We do not grasp its affirmations, its understanding of the meaning of Judaism if we look at it as merely a diminished form of the tradition. For at its center, Reform Judaism is an alternative expression of the tradition and not a watering down.

What is it that Reform affirms? It is the messianic hope, brave to be sure, in modern language. Let us listen to an expression of that hope, by Levi A. Olan:

> The faith of a liberal is undying. The periodic eruptions by reactionary movements have not extinguished the flame. Liberalism is essentially optimistic as it is practically progressive. It stakes its life upon the guarantee of a meaningful universe possessed of a God who assures the success of man's sincere efforts towards Him. If, at this moment in history, the forces of darkness are rampant, the liberal sets about to sharpen his weapons and reaffirms his determination. With certain ideas a liberal cannot compromise. That man is free to search and know God cannot be compromised no matter what the cost. That the universe will sustain man's highest hopes for the ultimate good cannot be compromised. The religion of the liberal is a fighting faith that draws its strength from the assurance that is given by the integrity and potentiality of the cosmic affirmation.[2]

This, I maintain, is no more than a modern way of saying what Jews in the first century said: I hope and believe that out of the present anguish a better day will come.

We have spoken about Reform Judaism. What do we mean by Reform Judaism? To answer that question we turn to a statement of the movement's guiding principles issued in 1937 by the Reform Rabbinical Organization, the Central Conference of American Rabbis.

i. *Judaism and Its Foundations*

1. *Nature of Judaism.* Judaism is the historical religious experience of the Jewish people. Though growing out of Jewish life, its message is universal, aiming at the union and perfection of mankind under the sovereignty of God. Reform Judaism recognizes the principle of progressive development in religion and consciously applies this principle to spiritual as well as to cultural and social life.

Judaism welcomes all truth, whether written in the pages of Scripture or deciphered from the records of nature. The new discoveries of science, while replacing the older scientific views underlying our sacred literature, do not conflict with the essential spirit of religion as manifested in the consecration of man's will, heart and mind to the service of God and of humanity.

2. *God.* The heart of Judaism and its chief contribution to religion is the doctrine of the One, living God, Who rules the world through law and love. In Him all existence has its creative source and mankind its ideal of conduct. Though transcending time and space, He is the indwelling Presence of the world. We worship Him as the Lord of the Universe and as our merciful Father.

3. *Man.* Judaism affirms that man is created in the Divine image. His spirit is immortal. He is an active co-worker with God. As a child of God, he is endowed with moral freedom and is charged with the responsibility of overcoming evil and striving after ideal ends.

4. *Torah.* God reveals Himself not only in the majesty, beauty and orderliness of nature, but also in the vision and moral striving of the human spirit. Revelation is a continuous process, confined to no one group and to no one age. Yet the people of Israel, through its prophets and sages, achieved unique insight in the realm of religious truth. The Torah, both written

and oral, enshrines Israel's ever-growing consciousness of God and of the moral law. It preserves the historical precedents, sanctions and norms of Jewish life, and seeks to mold it in the patterns of goodness and of holiness. Being products of historical processes, certain of its laws have lost their binding force with the passing of the conditions that called them forth. But as a depository of permanent spiritual ideals, the Torah remains the dynamic source of the life of Israel. Each age has the obligation to adapt the teaching of the Torah to its needs in consonance with the genius of Judaism.

5. *Israel.* Judaism is the soul of which Israel is the body. Living in all parts of the world, Israel has been held together by the ties of a common history, and above all, by the heritage of faith. Though we recognize in the group-loyalty of Jews who have become estranged from our religious tradition a bond which still unites them with us, we maintain that it is by its religion and for its religion that the Jewish people have lived. The non-Jew who accepts our faith is welcome as a full member of the Jewish community.

In all lands where our people live, they assume and seek to share loyally the full duties and responsibilities of citizenship and to create seats of Jewish knowledge and religion. In the rehabilitation of Palestine, the land hallowed by memories and hopes, we behold the promise of renewed life for many of our brethren. We affirm the obligation of all Jewry to aid in its upbuilding as a Jewish homeland by endeavoring to make it not only a haven of refuge for the oppressed but also a center of Jewish culture and spiritual life.

Throughout the ages it has been Israel's mission to witness to the Divine in the face of every form of paganism and materialism. We regard it as our historic task to cooperate with all men in the establishment of the kingdom of God, of universal brotherhood, justice, truth and peace on earth. This is our Messianic Goal.

ii. *Ethics*

6. *Ethics and Religion.* In Judaism religion and mo-

rality blend into an indissoluble unity. Seeking God means to strive after holiness, righteousness and goodness. The love of God is incomplete without the love of one's fellowmen. Judaism emphasizes the kinship of the human race, the sanctity and worth of human life and personality and the right of the individual to freedom and to the pursuit of his chosen vocation. Justice to all, irrespective of race, sect or class is the inalienable right and the inescapable obligation of all. The state and organized government exist in order to further these ends.

7. *Social Justice.* Judaism seeks the attainment of a just society by the application of its teachings to the economic order, to industry and commerce, and to national and international affairs. It aims at the elimination of man-made misery and suffering, poverty and degradation, of tyranny and slavery, of social inequality and prejudice, of ill-will and strife. It advocates the promotion of harmonious relations between warring classes on the basis of equality and justice, and the creation of conditions under which human personality may flourish. It pleads for the safeguarding of childhood against exploitation. It champions the cause of all who work and of their right to an adequate standard of living, as prior to the rights of property. Judaism emphasizes the duty of charity, and strives for a social order which will protect men against disabilities of old age, sickness and unemployment.

8. *Peace.* Judaism, from the days of the prophets, has proclaimed to mankind the ideal of universal peace. The spiritual and physical disarmament of all nations has been one of its essential teachings. It abhors all violence and relies upon moral education, love and sympathy to secure human progress. It regards justice as the foundation of the well-being of nations and the condition of enduring peace. It urges organized international action for disarmament, collective security and world peace.

iii. *Religious Practice*

9. *The Religious Life.* Jewish life is marked by conse-

cration to thse ideals of Judaism. It calls for faithful
participation in the life of the Jewish community as it
finds expression in home, synagogue and school and in
all other agencies that enrich Jewish life and promote its
welfare.

The Home has been and must continue to be a
stronghold of Jewish life, hallowed by the spirit of love
and reverence, by moral discipline and religious observance and worship.

The Synagogue is the oldest and most democratic
institution in Jewish life. It is the prime communal
agency by which Judaism is fostered and preserved. It
links the Jews of each community and unites them with
all Israel.

The perpetuation of Judaism as a living force depends
upon religious knowledge and upon the education of
each new generation in our rich cultural and spiritual
heritage.

Prayer is the voice of religion, the language of faith
and aspiration. It directs man's heart and mind God-
ward, voices the needs and hopes of the community,
and reaches out after goals which invest life with
supreme value. To deepen the spiritual life of our
people, we must cultivate the traditional habit of
communion with God through prayer in both home and
synagogue.

Judaism as a way of life requires, in addition to its
moral and spiritual demands, the preservation of the
Sabbath, festivals and Holy Days, the retention and
development of such customs, symbols and ceremonies
as possess inspirational value, the cultivation of distinctive forms of religious art and music and the use of
Hebrew, together with the vernacular, in our worship
and instruction.

These timeless aims and ideals of our faith we present
to a confused and troubled world. We call upon our
fellow Jews to rededicate themselves to them, and, in
harmony with all men, hopefully and courageously to
continue Israel's eternal quest after God and His
kingdom.

What is the emphasis of the guiding principles? It is on progress, history, the movement of humankind toward a better day. The most important paragraph from the viewpoint of our analysis is in part ii, under Ethics, number seven. The stress here, we can see, is on an optimistic goal, the achieving of a better age here on earth. Notice also the language at the end, speaking of Israel's eternal quest after God and His kingdom. Clearly, the rabbinic tradition will agree that what makes Reform Judaism truly new is its stress upon achieving that future now and by our own works.

The issue is not *whether* things change. The issue is whether change is good, leading toward something better. Abraham J. Feldman writes:

> Thus Reform is classical Judaism asserting anew the right and the duty of accelerating the process of progress and change where changes seem to be neces- sary. If some customs and practices are no longer mean- ingful, then they are no longer useful, and to cling to them mechanically or to acknowledge them as valid whilst they are largely neglected is to endanger the very survival of Jews and Judaism. In the absence of an authoritative legislative body continuing to function, and thus to be compelled to wait for the slow process of Halachic change through *responsa*, which often takes generations, is to expose the patient to danger. There- fore, Reform's principal contribution is the decision to keep Judaism forever contemporary, and to keep it responsive to the religious needs of successive genera- tions. Its purpose is not to preserve, let us say, in Hartford, or in Brooklyn, or in Chicago, or even in the United States of America, all the forms of the Judaism of Poland, of Galicia, Hungary, Rumania or Lithuania, but to keep Judaism *Jewish* in content whilst adapting the traditional forms to contemporary life, and creating new forms as needs require. Some day, Judaism in the State of Israel might become adapted to the new life and challenge of its needs and ways.
>
> Reform insists that changes be made *when* they are needed, *in* and *by* the generation that needs them,

rather than wait generations or even centuries before
any perceptible adjustments occur. Our generation
today and the generations tomorrow have the right and,
we think, the duty to keep Judaism alive by keeping it
contemporary, and responsive to their spiritual needs.
Our people can be Jewishly religious in America, for
example, without being coerced into irreligion by
attempting to mold American Jews into the religious
pattern or forms of Warsaw or Kovno or the Chief
Rabbis of Jerusalem. Reform in the United States has
undoubtedly saved hundreds of thousands of Jews for
Judaism and for Jewish life. Reform Judaism has saved
Jews for Judaism in America by making it possible and
proper to be religious Jews without strict and undeviat-
ing conformity to the minutiae of traditional practice.
To the extent that these Jews were saved for Jewish life,
Reform has made a vital contribution to all Jewish
religious life. It stemmed the tide of assimilation away
from Jewishness.[3]

Having defined Reform Judaism, let us now return to the
description of its place in modern Judaic religious life. We
notice that Reform Judaism is remarkably appropriate to the
condition of those Jews, living in Western countries and
enjoying political rights, who regarded the inherited mode of
Judaism as incongruous with their new situation.

Large numbers of Jews in the great cities of Germany and,
later on, in France, Britain, and the United States responded to
the new situation of Emancipation by acculturation. They
thereby sought to meet the requirements of the world to which
they supposed they were invited. Accepted as citizens, they
abandoned any pretense of separate nationality. Granted full
economic equality, they shaped their own economic ideals to
conform to those of the majority. They were desperately eager
to deserve the promises of cultural Emancipation. Like the
maskilim a generation or two earlier, they examined their cult
to discover those practices that were alien to the now interested
world, and determined to do away with them.

Reform Judaism proved to solve the problem of these
people. We must again stress that these were *not* Jews who
would choose the road to assimilation through conversion,

perfunctory or otherwise. They chose to remain Jews and retain Judaism. One might say they wanted to be Jews but not too "Jewish" — not so "Jewish" that they could not be citizens achieving a place in the undifferentiated society. This they wanted so badly that they saw and eagerly seized upon a welcome that few Gentiles, if any, really proffered.

The religious virtuosi who created Reform Judaism, those who had a better education, a richer family experience, a deeper involvement in the tradition to begin with, had the task of mediating between "the tradition" and the changes they saw about them and enthusiastically approved. For them, change became *Reform*. The direction of the people proved to be providential. As Solomon Freehof writes, "It was the Reformers who hailed the process and believed in it." They founded their reformation upon the concept that "essential Judaism" in its pure form required none of the measures that separated the Jew from other enlightened people, but consisted rather of beliefs and ethics, beliefs that were rational and destined in time to convince other sources. Freehof comments: "Reform Judaism is the first flaming up of direct world-idealism in Judaism since the days of Second Isaiah."

Isolating the prophets as the true exponents of Judaism, the Reformers chose within the messages of the prophets those texts that best served as useful pretexts for the liberalism of the age. The Reformers looked back upon the "golden age" when Judaism spoke to all humankind of the obligations of justice and mercy. It was that message that they saw to be "essential." All else was expendable. So the social ideals of the masses, who yearned for a liberal society in which even Jews would find acceptance, and those of "essential Judaism" were identical. The necessary changes would indeed constitute a reformation and a return to that time of the true and unadorned faith.

But more than this, the Reformers turned not only back to a golden age, but also forward to a golden age in the future, that time when bigotry and injustice would cease. They exhibited an idealism, an almost other-worldly confidence in humankind that suggests a radical disjuncture between their fantasies, on the one hand, and reality, on the other. The Jews were Europe's blacks, and Germany was their Mississippi or New York. They were excluded from the universities, ridiculed in the pulpits, libeled in the newspapers, insulted in private life. Yet they saw people as God's partners in the rebuilding of creation. They had the effrontery even to see themselves as bearers of a mission to humankind. God's Kingdom would be realized only through Judaism, "that most rational and ethical of all religions." The Jews had, they believed, an inherited, innate ability to give the world an ethical consciousness. In the symphony of nations — so common a metaphor in these decades — Jews would play the ethical melody.

Before we leave the topic of religious reform, let us consider the development of Modern, or Westernized Orthodoxy. This was an expression of Rabbinic Judaism that allowed for the acceptance of certain aspects of Western culture, while retaining the laws and religious perceptions of Rabbinic Judaism. The formation of this Westernized Orthodoxy should be understood as a creation of the Reformation, for only in response to the reformers did traditionalists self-consciously formulate what they regarded as orthodox *about* Judaism. Orthodox organizations were founded a half-century after the Reform movement took shape, not only in Germany, but in the United States. Orthodoxy, too, accepted the premises of the Reformation, that the Jews were going not only to live *among* Gentiles, but *with* them, and that therefore they had better learn the languages and adopt the culture, in its broadest form, of the West. But Orthodoxy determined on a different interpretation of what living with Gentiles must mean, a different ideal for modern Judaism. Orthodoxy stood for the tradition first, last, and always; it accepted, but only grudgingly affirmed, the conditions of modern life. Modernism was to be judged by the criterion of Torah, not the contrary. What was up-to-date was, standing by itself, no source of truth, let alone revelation.

Underlying this presupposition, nonetheless, is a vast reformation in traditional attitudes. Before the Jews could conceive themselves in such a new situation, they had to accept living with Gentiles as a good thing. They had to affirm it as the will of heaven, in a way in which they never had accepted or affirmed the high cultures of medieval and ancient times. Modernization long antedated both the modernist movement and its opposition. But the opposition at first was at a deep disadvantage, for it had to debate the issues already set by the Reformation, and to take a negative view where, in a more congenial situation, it might have found the grounds for affirming natural change as within the spirit of the Torah.

Favoring the Orthodox party were four factors. First was the natural conservatism of the religious Jew who followed not only the path of the Fathers, but the ways of the father himself. These ways were set by traditional parents who lent powerful psychic support to the Orthodox viewpoint.

Second, the Orthodox claimed that they represented the true and authentic Judaism. This claim was strengthened by the fact that the Orthodox were more like the preceding generations than were the Reformers. The Reformers' claim that they were "the true Judaism" had to be based upon a highly sophisticated, historicist argument that if the prophets or the Pharisees were alive in the nineteenth century, they would have been Reform Jews; therefore Reform Judaism was authentic, and Orthodoxy was not. But that argument persuaded only those who to begin with believed in it. For the rest, the claim of Orthodoxy to historical authenticity seemed reasonable, for it conformed to their own observations of religious life.

Third, the virtuosi of Reform were concerned for authenticity, but the Reform laymen were not. The Orthodox continued to attract those Jews most serious about Judaism. Orthodoxy therefore benefited from the high level of commitment of its lay men and women, people prepared to make every sacrifice for the faith. In a measure, Reform was attractive not only to reformers, but also to assimilationists. That is to say, whatever the virtuosi's intent, for the lay follower the Reform movement was a vehicle of his own convenience, used by the passenger to reach a point quite outside the itinerary of the driver.

Two sorts of Jews participated in the creation of the Reform movement. One was the virtuoso, the Jew who not only was raised in a traditional environment, but took seriously the propositions of the tradition, and therefore made changes on the basis of commitment and reflection. The other was the ordinary person who, while intending to remain a faithful Jew, could see no reason to preserve what he thought were outdated, "medieval," or simply outlandish habits of dress, nourishment, speech, prayer, and the like. For him the Reform movement offered a satisfactory way to continue within the Judaic faith; he felt not the slightest interest in rationalizations. Thus, for example, praying in the manner of Protestant Christians — in the vernacular, in decorous manner, with organ music and choirs, with men and women sitting together — had great appeal to a German Jew eager to find personal and religious acceptance among Gentiles. But those responsible for such changes needed to persuade themselves that greater, more solemn truths than merely aping the Gentile were expressed through the reform of the liturgy.

The fourth factor favoring Orthodoxy was that, as the Orthodox claim to constitute the one legitimate form of Judaism and to measure by itself the "authenticity" of all "deviant" forms developed, Orthodoxy came to offer a security and a certainty unavailable elsewhere. Its concept of a direct relationship between the individual's conformity to the tradition and the will of the Creator of the Universe bore a powerful attraction for those seeking a safe way in the world, those less concerned with the golden age to come, though still hoping for it.

Just as not all Europeans were liberals, so too not all Jews; not even most Jews in many places responded to the liberal message of the Reformation. And many who did were in time won back to the "tradition" — in its Central European "cultured" form to be sure — when Orthodoxy addressed itself to them in good German, rather than in good Yiddish. What some wanted was merely to dress like Gentiles and speak like them, but to live, nonetheless, by patterns they believed were revealed at Sinai. The achievement of the Orthodox thinkers was to offer reassurance that certain parts of life were truly neutral; but in so saying, they accomplished the grandest reformation of all.

Samson Raphael Hirsch (1808-1888), the chief spokesman for Western European Orthodoxy, was reared in Germany. His knowledge of the traditional sciences was acquired mainly through his own efforts. The chief influence on this thought about contemporary Judaism was Jacob Ettlinger, who stated, "Let not him who is engaged in the war of the Lord against the heretics be held back by the false argument that great is peace and that it is better to maintain the unity of all designated as Jews than to bring about disruption." Such an affirmation of the sectarian option represents a strange attitude indeed among those who would lay claim to "sole legitimacy." Hirsch, by contrast, in his *Nineteen Letters*, issued no threats of excommunication, but stressed the affirmative requirement to study the Torah, with the rationalistic, perhaps ironic, certainty that knowledge would yield assent, an optimism different in form but not in substance from that of the reformers. When he settled in Frankfurt, he found a community dominated by the Reformation. At his death, he left in it a bastion of Orthodoxy, originally established in separation from the "community" — that is, from the government-recognized *Community*, which was Reform.

Hirsch accomplished this radical change chiefly by founding a school. He designed the curriculum so that the next generation would conform to the ideal by which he lived: "Torah and *Derekh Eretz*," that is, traditional science combined with general secular enlightenment. Judaism, he held, "encompasses all of life, in the synagogue and in the kitchen . . . To be a Jew — in a life which in its totality is borne on the world of the Lord and is perfected in harmony with the will of God — this is the scope and goal of Judaism . . . Insofar as a Jew is a Jew, his views and objectives become universal. He will not be a stranger to anything which is good, true, and beautiful in art and in science, in civilization and in learning . . . He will hold firmly to this breadth of view in order to fulfill his mission as a Jew and to live up to the function of his Judaism in areas never imagined by his father."

Hirsch therefore proposed a model of "the Jewish-man," who fears God, keeps the commandments, and looks at the "wonders of the Lord in nature and the mighty deeds of the Lord in history." He added, however, that "Jewish-man" brings about not only the redemption of Israel, but also the redemption of all mankind. No less than the reformers', Hirsch's reformation spoke of a "mission of Israel," and aimed at the "redemption of mankind," both the hallmarks of the liberal, enlightened German of the day.

Both Reform and Orthodox Judaism represent, therefore, modes of response to modernization. For both the constants were Scriptures, concern for the religious dimension of existence, concentration upon the historical traditional sciences, though in different ways, and concern for the community of Jews. These persisted, but in new forms. Hirsch's "Torah and *Derekh Eretz*," no less than the "science of Judaism" (*Wissenschaft des Judentums*) produced within the Reform movement, constituted strikingly new approaches to the study of the Torah. The rhetoric of Israel's mission, now focusing in both movements upon the private person, reflected the new social datum of Jewish living — no longer as a nation but as individuals — and concealed, in both instances, the utter decay of the traditional social context. For both, concentration upon the community and its structures, policies, and future involved considerable use of sociological language. For neither were the traditional categories of covenant and sacred community any longer characteristic of a broad and catholic concern for *all* Jews in a given place. Both address themselves, because the times required it, to German- or French- or English-speaking Jews.

Neither Reform nor Orthodox Judaism could conceive of a parochial and self-sustaining language of Jewish discourse. Both spoke of a messianic mission of Israel to the world, and conceived of redemption in terms at least relevant to the Gentile. This is not to suggest that the tradition in its earlier formulations was here misrepresented; but both Orthodox and Reform Judaism were very different from contemporary, premodern, archaic Judaism in Eastern Europe, North Africa, and elsewhere. Both were far more sophisticated, intellectual, articulate, and self-conscious than traditional Judaisms outside Western Europe.

The religious virtuosi of Reform and Orthodoxy were already prepared for a new formulation of the tradition long before either Reform or Orthodoxy made an appearance. Indeed, in significant ways, both represent a very considerable lag. The rigidity of Orthodoxy, moreover, is peculiarly modern and was called forth by changes in the quality of the Jews' way of living. We can hardly locate, in earlier times, an equivalent rejection of contemporary learning. We can find only few premodern examples of such paralysis in the face of need to update legal doctrines. Quite obviously, it was a fearful inability to cope with changes which produced the claim that change was, for the most part, undesirable and even impossible. Change not only was *not* reform, it was the work of the devil. Similarly, the sectarianism of both Reform and Orthodox groups, their abandonment of the ambition to struggle with all Jews for the achievement of universal goals within a single, united community, constitutes a failure of nerve in the face of the diversities and inconstancies of the modern situation.

Zionism

If Reform Judaism took an optimistic view of the changes of modern times, Zionism, taking history as seriously as Reform, saw matters differently. Zionism came into being toward the end of the nineteenth century because of the profound disappointment of Western Jews at the growth of a new anti-Semitism. One of the most significant Jewish responses to modern nationalism, and the Jews' form of nationalism, Zionism began as a political movement. Yet it contained within itself a new interpretation of all the values of the rabbinic tradition and in important ways represented a fundamentally religious response to modern times, a response we call messianic.

If we look at the situation of the Jews from the 1840s to the 1870s, we find that they were making their way into Western society. In 1870 Disraeli, identified as a Jew although converted to Christianity, was in power in England. The German labor movement was in the process of formation by important Jewish labor leaders. Jews were sitting in the Prussian Parliament. Throughout Western Europe it seemed clear that the promises of reform and political emancipation would be kept. Anti-Semitism was scarcely an issue facing European Jewry in the 1860s. Thirty years later, by contrast, anti-Semitism was a major factor in European politics and culture. During the intervening thirty years the doctrine had grown up and been accepted that all that was wrong in Europe was caused by the Jews. Hatred of the Jews was raised to a metaphysical level: They were seen as agents of change, as hostile to nationalism, as the enemy of civilization.

For example, the German composer Richard Wagner said that what is needed is not a revolution to enthrone the abstract idea of human quality, but a revolution to release the forces of racial authenticity from the inhibiting, distorting influences of Judaic-Christian-rationalist universalism and materialism. The Jews were blamed for economic crisis as much as for cultural change. A racial theory grew up which stressed blood and unconscious reflexes, and linked race to the organic pattern of life. The obsession of the prophets of race was with the decay of culture and the doom of civilization. Darwin's theory, that of a struggle for survival, was linked to society. Races are not equal. They struggle with one another for life. The strongest race will survive.

The Jews were singled out as outsiders and as an inferior race. They were given two contradictory roles. First, they were seen as a kind of antirace, as international and cosmopolitan. But, second, they were seen as a racial group that was clannish and cohesive and determined to rule the world. This was a contradictory fantasy.

Anti-Semitism at this time must not be understood as a kind of social exclusion but as an expression of a total world view. Political parties were organized with anti-Semitism as the center of the program. These parties claimed to defend the national spirit against Jewish cosmopolitanism. Anti-Semitism became a world view, a religion, an alternative to the Enlightenment.

Zionism was born as a political movement among the Jews to create a Jewish state in response to the hopelessness of the European situation. The movement was founded by Theodor Herzl in the last decade of the nineteenth century as a solution to "the Jewish question." In his *The Jewish State*, Herzl wrote about the Jewish question:

> No one can deny the gravity of the Jewish situation. Wherever they live in appreciable number, Jews are persecuted in greater or lesser measure. Their equality before the law, granted by statute, has become practically a dead letter. They are debarred from filling even moderately high offices in the army, or in any public or private institutions. And attempts are being made to thrust them out of business also: "Don't buy from Jews!"
>
> Attacks in parliaments, in assemblies, in the press, in the pulpit, in the street, on journeys — for example, their exclusion from certain hotels — even in places of recreation are increasing from day to day. The forms of persecutions vary according to country and social circle.

In Russia, special taxes are levied on Jewish villages; in Romania, a few persons are put to death; in Germany, they get a good beating occasionally; in Austria, anti-Semites exercise their terrorism over all public life; in Algeria, there are traveling agitators; in Paris, the Jews are shut out of the so-called best social circles and excluded from clubs. The varieties of anti-Jewish expression are innumerable. But this is not the occasion to attempt the sorry catalogue of Jewish hardships. We shall not dwell on particular cases, however painful.

I do not aim to arouse sympathy on our behalf. All that is nonsense, as futile as it is dishonorable. I shall content myself with putting the following questions to the Jews: Is it not true that, in countries where we live in appreciable numbers, the position of Jewish lawyers, doctors, technicians, teachers, and employees of every description becomes daily more intolerable? Is it not true that the Jewish middle classes are seriously threatened? Is it not true that the passions of the mob are incited against our wealthy? Is it not true that our poor endure greater suffering than any other proletariat? I think that this pressure is everywhere present. In our upper economic classes it causes discomfort, in our middle classes utter despair.

The fact of the matter is, everything tends to one and the same conclusion, which is expressed in the classic Berlin cry: "Juden 'raus!'" ("Out with the Jews!").

I shall now put the question in the briefest possible form: Shouldn't we "get out" at once, and if so, whither?

Or, may we remain, and if so, how long?

Let us first settle the point of remaining. Can we hope for better days, can we possess our souls in patience, can be wait in pious resignation till the princes and peoples of this earth are more mercifully disposed toward us? I say that we cannot hope for the current shift. And why not? Even if we were as near to the hearts of princes as are their other subjects, they could not protect us. They would only incur popular hatred by showing us too much favor. And this "too much" implies less than is claimed as a right by any ordinary citizen or ethnic group. The nations in whose midst Jews live are all covertly or openly anti-Semitic.

The common people have not, and indeed cannot have, any comprehension of history. They do not know that the sins of the Middle Ages are now being visited on the nations of Europe. We are what the ghetto made us. We have without a doubt attained pre-eminence in finance because medieval conditions drove us to it. The same process is now being repeated. We are again being forced into money-lending — now named stock exchange — by being kept out of other occupations. But once on the stock exchange, we are again objects of contempt. At the same time we continue to produce an abundance of mediocre intellectuals who find no outlet, and this endangers our social position as much as does our increasing wealth. Educated Jews without means are now rapidly becoming socialists. Hence we are certain to suffer acutely in the struggle between the classes, because we stand in the most exposed position in both the capitalist and the socialist camps.[4]

Zionism as a political movement supplied a close analysis of the causes of anti-Semitism as well as a program for the solution to the Jewish problem. Herzl's analysis of the causes of anti-Semitism is as follows:

We now no longer discuss the irrational causes, prejudice and narrow-mindedness, but the political and economic causes. Modern anti-Semitism is not to be confused with the persecution of the Jews in former times, though it does still have a religious aspect in some countries. The main current of Jew-hatred is today a different one. In the principal centers of anti-Semitism, it is an outgrowth of the emancipation of the Jews. When civilized nations awoke to the inhumanity of discriminatory legislation and enfranchised us, our enfranchisement came too late. Legislation alone no longer sufficed to emancipate us in our old homes. For in the ghetto we had remarkably developed into a bourgeois people and we emerged from the ghetto a prodigious rival to the middle class. Thus we found ourselves thrust, upon emancipation, into this bourgeois circle, where we have a double pressure to sustain, from within and from without. The Christian bourgeoisie would indeed not be loath to cast us as a peace offering to socialism, little though that would avail them.

At the same time, the equal rights of Jews before the law cannot be rescinded where they have once been granted. Not only because their recision would be contrary to the spirit of our age, but also because it would immediately drive all Jews, rich and poor alike, into the ranks of the revolutionary parties. No serious harm can really be done us. In olden days our jewels were taken from us. How is our movable property to be seized now? It consists of printed papers which are locked up somewhere or other in the world, perhaps in the strongboxes of Christians. It is, of course, possible to get at railway shares and debentures, banks and industrial undertakings of all descriptions, by taxation; and where the progressive income tax is in force all our movable property can eventually be laid hold of. But all these efforts cannot be directed against Jews alone, and wherever they might nevertheless be made, their upshot would be immediate economic crises, which would by no means be confined to the Jews as the first affected. The very impossibility of getting at the Jews nourishes and deepens hatred of them. Anti-Semitism increases day by day and hour by hour among the nations; indeed, it is bound to increase, because the causes of its growth continue to exist and are ineradicable. Its remote cause is the loss of our assimilability during the Middle Ages; its immediate cause is our excessive production of mediocre intellectuals, who have no outlet downward or upward — or rather, no wholesome outlet in either direction. When we sink, we become a revolutionary proletariat, the corporals of every revolutionary party; and when we rise, there rises also our terrifying financial power.[5]

Thus far you must wonder why it is that Zionism enters a discussion of modern Judaism. It seems an entirely this-worldly

and secular phenomenon. But what Zionism proposes as a
solution to secular Jewish problems rapidly becomes a movement endowed in the imagination of its followers with
profound messianic consequences. This solution was to found a
Jewish state. The eventual response of the Jewish people was to
see the program of Zionism, and later the State of Israel, as
much more than a secular solution to a this-worldly problem.
Rather what was and is perceived was the beginning of
redemption, the messianic restoration of the Jewish people to
the land about which we read in the prayers. In other words the
appeal of Zionism was to those very messianic symbols, that
exact messianic program of the tradition itself. Rabbi Arthur
Hertzberg writes:

> Zionism is Jewish messianism in process of realizing
> itself through this-worldly means. This description fits
> that stream of Zionist thought which remained ortho-
> dox in religious outlook, and therefore limited its
> tinkering with the classical messianic conception of the
> Jewish religion to the question of means; but this thesis
> pretends to apply to the main body of the movement,
> and, as such, it is artificial and evasive. What is being
> obscured is the crucial problem of modern Zionist
> ideology, the tension between the inherited messianic
> concept and the radically new meaning that Zionism, at
> its most modern, was proposing to give it.
>
> Religious messianism had always imagined the
> Redemption as a confrontation between the Jew and
> God. The Gentile played a variety of roles in this
> drama — as chastising rod in the divine hand, as the
> enemy to be discomfited, or, at very least, as the
> spectator to pay homage at the end of the play — but
> none of these parts are indispensable to the plot. In the
> cutting edge of Zionism, in its most revolutionary
> expression, the essential dialogue is now between the
> Jew and the nations of the earth. What marks modern
> Zionism as a fresh beginning in Jewish history is that its
> ultimate values derive from the general milieu. The
> Messiah is now identified with the dream of an age of
> individual liberty, national freedom, and economic and
> social justice — i.e., with the progressive faith of the
> nineteenth century.

This is the true Copernican revolution which modern Zionism announced — and it patently represents a fundamental change not merely in the concept of the means to the Redemption but in end values. Every aspect of Jewish messianism has been completely transmuted by this new absolute. So, classical Judaism had, for the most part, imagined that at some propitious moment an inner turning by the Chosen People would be the preamble to evoking the saving grace of God. Zionism, too, knows that the Jewish people must be remade in order to be redeemed — indeed, its sweeping and passionate demands lent themselves to being spoken in language reminiscent of the prophets (thus providing one of the several bridges between the old and the new) — but it is supremely aware that its millennium is out of reach without the ascent and cooperation of the dominant political powers. In the movement's heroic age, therefore, Theodor Herzl made the international scene his primary area and spent his career, often in pathos and tragedy, in searching for a likely ally in the antechambers of the potentates. Having embarked on the quest for a Jewish kingdom of this world, Zionism perforce had to address itself to the keeper of the keys to that kingdom, the Gentile. Or, to state the point from a wider perspective, the scheme of Jewish religion had seen the messianic problem as one of resolving the tension between the Jew and his Maker — the Exile is punishment and atonement for sin; for the new doctrine, at its newest, the essential issue is the end of the millennia of struggle between the Jew and the world.

The secularization of the messianic ideal called into question another of the basic concepts of Judaism, the notion of the "chosen people." Modern Zionism agreed with the classical faith that the Jews had once been chosen to lead the world, and, in this connection, it was not important whether it was believed that the choosing had been done by God or by the unique Jewish national genius. However, one question, that of the place of the Jew in the postmessianic era, could not be avoided. Despite some occasional remarks to the contrary, the weight of learned opinion in the authoritative religious writings and the whole of popular Jewish feeling had always been certain that the election of the Jew would persist to all eternity. This idea has been no problem to those who combined the older pieties with their Zionism, who have therefore simply accepted it, or to the unflinching secularists and humanists, who have completely discarded it. But the mainstream of the movement has not really known what to do with the idea of the "chosen people." If the new messianism meant the normalization of the place of the Jew in the world, what unique destiny was ultimately reserved for him? If his "end of days" is to be an honorable and secure share in the larger liberal society of the future, what remains of his "chosenness?"[6]

It is clear from Rabbi Hertzberg's words that Zionism is a mode of Judaism, a messianic mode, as much as Reform is a messianic mode. As we observed earlier what the two have in common is a very simple attitude, that the events of the day and age are important and — even more consequential — are leading somewhere.

This view, that Jews have to confront not only the condition of the Jewish people but the condition of Judaism itself, is most clearly stated by another Zionist, Ahad Ha-Am. He saw most clearly the meaning of Zionism and the problem facing Judaism. He distinguished between the political and social problem of the Jews, and the problem of Judaism. He said:

It is not only the Jews who have come out of the ghetto; Judaism has come out, too. For the Jews the exodus from the ghetto is confined to certain countries and is due to toleration; but Judaism has come out (or is coming out) of its own accord, wherever it has come into contact with modern culture. This contact with modern culture overturns the inner defenses of Judaism, so that it can no longer remain isolated and live a life apart. The spirit of our people desires further development; it wants to absorb the basic elements of general culture which are reaching it from the outside world, to digest them and to make them a part of itself, as it has done before at various periods of its history. But the conditions of its life in exile are not suitable for such a task. In our time culture expresses itself everywhere through the form of the national spirit, and the stranger who would become part of culture must sink his individuality and become absorbed in the dominant environment. In exile, Judaism cannot, therefore, develop its individuality in its own way. When it leaves the ghetto walls, it is in danger of losing its essential being, or — at very least — its national unity; it is in danger of being split up into as many kinds of Judaism, each with a different character and life, as there are countries of the dispersion.[7]

Ahad Ha-Am focuses as do the Reformers upon the issues of Judaism. He offers as an ideal the message of the prophets:

The secret of our people's persistence is — as I have tried to show elsewhere — that at a very early period the Prophets taught us to respect only the power of the spirit and not to worship material power. Therefore, unlike the other nations of antiquity, the Jewish people never reached the point of losing its self-respect in the face of more powerful enemies. As long as we remain faithful to this principle, our existence has a secure basis, and we shall not lose our self-respect, for we are not spiritually inferior to any nation. But a political ideal which is not grounded in our national culture is apt to seduce us from loyalty to our own inner spirit and to beget in us a tendency to find the path of glory in the attainment of material power and political dominion, thus breaking the thread that unites us with the past and undermining our historical foundation. Needless to say, if the political ideal is not attained, it will have disastrous consequences, because we shall have lost the old basis without finding a new one. But even if it is attained under present conditions, when we are a scattered people not only in the physical but also in the spiritual sense — even then, Judaism will be in great danger. Almost all our great men — those, that is, whose education and social position have prepared them to be at the head of a Jewish State — are spiritually far removed from Judaism and have no true conception of its nature and its value. Such men, however loyal to

their State and devoted to its interests, will necessarily
envisage those interests by the standards of the foreign
culture which they themselves have imbibed; and they
will endeavor, by moral persuasion or even by force, to
implant that culture in the Jewish State, so that in the
end the Jewish State will be a State of Germans or
Frenchmen of the Jewish race. We have even now a
small example of this process in Palestine.

What then is the importance of Zionism in relation to
Messianic Judaism? The Jews sustained the hope of returning to
the homeland, and the very heart of their messianic belief, its
symbols and fantasies, were shaped by that hope. Some Jews
always remained in the land of Israel, but all Jews until the
nineteenth century expected to assemble to witness the
resurrection of the dead there. Judaic Messianism was, as
Professor Joseph L. Blau emphasizes, invariably supposed to be
a political phenomenon by contrast to the restorationism of
non-Jews, in which Zion was in heaven, not on earth. William
Blake's "Jerusalem" could perhaps be built in England; the Zion
of Jewish piety could *only* be the earthly, specific place. For
this reason the early Reformers found traditional Messianism an
embarrassment.

When Napoleon asked the French Rabbinical Sanhedrin of
1807, "Do those Jews who are born in France . . . regard France
as their native country?" the answer of the rabbis could only
have been in the affirmative. Yet such an answer could not
possibly be a true one, except during the Reformation. Ludwig
Philippson wrote, "Formerly the Jews had striven to create a
nation . . . but now their goal was to join other nations . . . It
was the task of the new age to form a general human society
which would encompass all peoples organically. In the same
way, it was the task of the Jews not to create their own
nation . . . but rather to obtain from the other nations full
acceptance into their society." Similarly, the West London
Synagogue of British Jews heard from its first rabbi in 1845,
"To this land [England] we attach ourselves with a patriotism
as glowing, with a devotion as fervent, and with a love as ardent
and sincere as any class of our British non-Jewish fellow
citizens." One could duplicate that statement, and with it, its
excessive protest, many times.

The Reformation emphasized that Judaism could eliminate

the residue of its nationalistic phase that survived in traditional doctrine and liturgy. The Reformers saw Messianism not as Zionist doctrine, but as a call to the golden age in which a union of nations into one peaceful realm to serve their one true God would take place. The happy optimism that underlay these hopes and affirmations survived among some even after Auschwitz.

But for the assimilated Western Jews of Paris, Vienna, and London, the rise of virulent scientific and political anti-Semitism during the last third of the nineteenth century raised significant doubts. Nor did the political situation of Eastern European Jewry, characterized by pogroms, repression, and outright murder, provide reassurance. Humankind did not seem to be progressing very quickly toward that golden day.

Modern Zionism, the movement to establish a Jewish state in Palestine, thus represented a peculiar marriage of Western romantic nationalism and Eastern Jewish piety. The virtuosi of the movement were mostly Western, but the masses of followers were in the East. Fustel de Coulanges's saying, "True patriotism is not love of the soil, but love of the past, reverence for the generations which have preceded us," at once excluded Jews, who were newcomers to French culture and could hardly share love for a French past that included banishment of their ancestors, and invited some of them to rediscover their own patriotism, Zionism. The Jews could not share the "collective being"; they could not be absorbed into a nation whose national past they did not share. The Dreyfus trial of 1893-94 forced upon the Viennese reporter, Theodor Herzl, whose Zionist proposal we read, a clear apprehension that the "Jewish problem" could be solved only by complete assimilation or complete evacuation. It occurred to no one in the West that extermination was an option, though the Czarist Russians thought of it.

In response to the Dreyfus trial, Herzl published *Der Judenstaat (The Jewish State)*, from whose appearance in 1896 is conventionally dated the foundation of modern Zionism. One can hardly overemphasize the secularity of Herzl's vision. He did not appeal to religious sentiments, but to modern secular nationalism. His view of anti-Semitism, as we saw, ignores the religious dimension altogether, but stresses only economic and social causes. Modern anti-Semitism grows out of the emancipation of the Jews and their entry into competition with the middle classes. The Jews cannot cease to exist as Jews, for affliction increases their cohesiveness.

Herzl's solution was wholly practical: Choose a country to which Jews could go, perhaps Argentina, or Uganda, which was made available by the British government a few years later. What was important was a rational plan: The poor would go first and build the infrastructure of an economy; the middle classes would follow to create trade, markets, and new opportunity. The first Zionist Congress was not a gathering of Messianists, but of sober men and women. Herzl's statement, "At Basel I founded the Jewish state," was not, however, a sober statement, nor was his following one, "The State is already founded in essence, in the will of the people of the State." According to Herzl, all that remained were mere practicalities.

Herzl's disciple, Max Nordau, held that Zionism resulted from nationalism and anti-Semitism. Had Zionism led to a Jewish state in Uganda, one could have believed it. But when Herzl proposed Uganda, he was defeated. The masses in the East had been heard from. They bitterly opposed any "Zion" but Jerusalem. To them, Zionism could mean only Zion. Jerusalem was in one place alone. The classical messianic language, much of which was already associated with Zion in the messianic era, was taken over by the Zionist movement, and evoked a much more than political response in Jewish hearts. Zionism swept the field, and in the twentieth century even the Reform movement affirmed it and contributed some of its major leaders. Only small groups within Reform and Orthodoxy resisted, the latter because they saw Zionism as an act of pride, contravening the hope in supernatural Messianism.

Calling a land-colonization fund, known in English as the Jewish National Fund, by the Hebrew words, *Keren Kayemet Le-Yisrael* — the "Eternal Fund of Israel" — was a deliberate effort to evoke the Talmudic *Keren Kayemet le-Olam HaBa*, "Eternal Fund for the World to Come," which consisted of acts of merit, piety, or charity, destined to produce a heavenly reward. To the doggedly religious ear such a title was nothing less than blasphemy, for it made use of sacred language in a secular sense. But that represents the very ambiguity of Zionism, a strange marriage between Western assimilated leaders on the one hand, and Eastern traditionalists on the other.

The history of Zionism has not here been adumbrated, let alone exhausted; but for our purposes, its pecularity has become clear. As Rabbi Hertzberg states, "Zionism cannot be typed, and therefore easily explained as a 'normal' kind of national risorgimento [reorganization] . . . From the Jewish perspective, messianism, and not nationalism, is the primary element in Zionism . . . Writers too numerous to mention here have characterized the modern movement as 'secular messianism,' to indicate at once what is classical in Zionism — its eschatological purpose; and what is modern — the necessarily contemporary tools of political effort." Hertzberg rejects this characterization as too simple. Rather he sees as the crucial problem of Zionist ideology "the tension between the inherited messianic concept and the radically new meaning that Zionism, at its most modern, was proposing to give it."

Hertzberg's analysis is very searching, but I believe it is precisely this tension that is meant by those who have seen Zionism as a modernized, if not wholly secularized, messianism. Hertzberg greatly deepens the discussion when he says that the crisis is "not solely in the means but in the essential meaning of Jewish messianism . . . it is the most radical attempt in Jewish history to break out of the parochial molds of Jewish life in order to become part of the general history of man in the modern world. Hence we are face to face with a paradoxical truth: For the general historian, Zionism is not easy to deal with because it is too 'Jewish'; the Jewish historian finds it hard to define because it is too general."

But so far as Zionism aspired to create a state like other states and to "normalize" the existence of the Jews, it represented a massive movement toward assimilation. Its goal was to end the particular and peculiar Judaic way of living and to substitute for it the commonplace and universal modern mode of life. And it succeeded. So, while expressive of the unique and special aspects of Judaic messianism and bound up with the most private hopes of Jewry, it served, in a paradoxical way, as the means for ending the unique and making public what had been private. In creating the largest Jewish neighborhood in the world, where Jews lose a sense of being different, it refocused the center of Judaic existence away from its parochial mold and placed the Jews within the mainstream of international life.

Thus far in our consideration of Zionism, we have ignored its limited importance as a minority movement in the public life of world Jewry before World War II. The Zionist movements in various countries by no means encompassed the majority of the Jewish population, and Zionist efforts at raising funds for the purchase of land in Palestine and for the settlement of Jewish men and women on the land did not receive the support of the larger number of Jews in the Diaspora. So while we have stressed the messianic character of Zionist thought, we also must emphasize the limited appeal, before Hitler, of that messianic and practical enterprise. What transformed Zionism from a limited to a universal movement, affecting the imagination and guiding the public actions and aspirations of nearly the whole Jewish people, was the extermination of European Jewry between 1933 and 1945. It was at that moment that the messianic promise of Zionism became the sole hope left for Jewry. When the full weight of the extermination of European Jewry became known and felt, after 1945, the old and natural question, *Oh Lord, how long?* had one answer only, *Until Zion.* The messianic movement took shape before the hour of its fulfillment. When the time came, Zionism presented the sole meaningful answer. It was that ineluctable, if tragic, fittingness of Zionism to the Holocaust which, for a while, turned Judaism once more into a messianic religion and forced the events of the moment, the practical and political happenings of the day, constantly upon the attention of Judaists, among all Jews. Let us now consider the human realities shaped by the Holocaust and given meaning by Zionism.

The Holocaust

Between 1933 and 1945 nearly six million Jews, the mass of the Jewish community in all of Europe, were exterminated.

The events of 1933 and 1948 constitute one of the decisive moments in the history of Judaism, to be compared in their far-reaching effects to the destruction of the First and Second Temples, in 586 B.C.E., and 70 C.E.; the massacres of Rhineland Jewries in 1096; the aftermath of the Black Plague in 1349; the expulsion of the Jews from Spain in 1492; or the Ukrainian massacres of 1648-9. But while the Jews responded to those disasters in essentially religious ways, the response to the Holocaust and the creation of the State of Israel has not on the surface been religious. That is to say, while in the past people explained disaster as a result of sin and therefore sought means of reconciliation with God and atonement, in the twentieth century the Jews superficially did not. Instead they performed what seem secular, and not religious, deeds: They raised money, engaged in political action, and did all the other things modern, secular people, confident they can cope with anything, normally do. They did not write new prayers or holy books, create new theologies, or develop new religious ideas and institutions.

Yet the response to the Holocaust and the creation of the State of Israel differs in form, not in substance, from earlier response to disaster. The form now is secular. The substance endures in deeply religious ways. For the affect of the Holocaust and the creation of the State of Israel on the Jews is to produce a new myth — by myth, I mean a transcendent perspective on events, a story lending meaning and imparting sanctity to ordinary, everyday actions — and a new religious affirmation.

Let me recount the salvific story as it is nearly universally perceived by the senior generation of American Jews — those who came to maturity before 1945. This is how I should tell the story:

"Once upon a time, when I was a young man, I felt helpless before the world. I was a Jew, when being Jewish was a bad thing. As a child, I saw my old Jewish parents, speaking a foreign language and alien in countless ways, isolated from America. And I saw America, dimly perceived to be sure, exciting and promising, but hostile to me as a Jew. I could not get into a good college. I could not aspire to medical school. I could not become an architect or an engineer. I could not even work for an electric utility.

"When I took my vacation, I could not go just anywhere, but had to ask whether Jews would be welcomed, tolerated, embarrassed, or thrown out. Being Jewish was uncomfortable. Yet I could not give it up. My mother and my father had made me what I was. I could hide, but could not wholly deny, to myself if not to others, that I was a Jew. And I could not afford the price in diminished self-esteem, of opportunity denied, aspiration deferred and insult endured. Above all, I saw myself as weak and pitiful. I could not do anything about being a Jew nor could I do much to improve my lot as a Jew.

"Then came Hitler and I saw that what was my private lot was the dismal fate of every Jew. Everywhere Jew hatred was raised from the gutter to the heights. Not from Germany alone, but from people I might meet at work or in the streets I learned that being Jewish was a metaphysical evil. 'The Jews' were not accepted, but debated. Friends would claim we were not all bad. Enemies said we were. And we had nothing to say at all.

"As I approached maturity, a still more frightening fact confronted me. People guilty of no crime but Jewish birth were forced to flee their homeland and no one would accept them. Ships filled with ordinary men, women and children searched the oceans for a safe harbor. And I and they had nothing in common but one fact, and that fact made all else inconsequential. Had I been there, I should have been among them. I too should not have been saved at the sea.

"Then came the war and, in its aftermath, the revelation of the shame and horror of holocaust, the decay and corrosive hopelessness of the DP camps, the contempt of the nations, who would neither accept nor help the saved remnants of hell.

"At the darkest hour came the dawn. The State of Israel saved the remnant and gave meaning and significance to the inferno. After the dawn, the great light: Jews no longer helpless, weak, unable to decide their own fate, but strong, confident, decisive."

This constitutes the myth that gives meaning and transcendence to the conventional lives of ordinary people — the myth of the darkness followed by light, of passage through the netherworld and past the gates of hell, then, purified by suffering and by blood, into the new age. The naturalist myth of American Jewry — it is not the leaders' alone — conforms to the supernatural structure of the classic myths of salvific religions from time immemorial. And well it might, for a salvific myth has to tell the story of sin and redemption, disaster and salvation, the old being and the new, the vanquishing of death and mourning, crying and pain, the passing away of former things. The vision of the new Jerusalem, complete in 1967, beckoned not tourists, but pilgrims, to the new heaven and the new earth. This, as I said, is the myth that shapes the mind and imagination of

American Jewry, supplies the correct interpretation and denotes the true significance of everyday events, and turns workaday people into saints. This is the myth that transforms common-place affairs into history, turns making a donation to the State of Israel into a sacred act.

It is not faith, theology, or ideology. It is myth in that it so closely corresponds to, and yet so magically transforms and elevates, reality, that people take vision and interpretation for fact. They do not need to believe in, or affirm the myth, for they know it to be true. In that they are confident of the exact correspondence between reality and the story that explains reality, they are the saved, the saints, the witnesses to the end of days: "We know this is how things really were, and what they really meant. We know it because the myth of suffering and redemption corresponds to our perceptions of reality, evokes immediate recognition and assent. It not only bears meaning, it imparts meaning precisely because it explains experience and derives from what we know to be true."

We see therefore that the messianic myth of Zionism was able to impart meaning to the Holocaust. Let us now turn to the impact of the Holocaust upon Jewish theology. We shall see that two responses to the religious meaning of the Holocaust embody the two forms of Judaism we discerned at the very outset, Messianic Judaism and Rabbinic Judaism.

Two significant names, Richard L. Rubenstein and Emil Fackenheim, normally are associated with the theological impact of the Holocaust and the rise of the State of Israel. Rubenstein's response to the Holocaust has been searching and courageous. He has raised difficult questions and responded with painful honesty. The consequence has been an unprecedented torrent of personal abuse, so that he has nearly been driven out of Jewish public life. He has been called a Nazi and compared to Hitler. The abuse to which he has been subjected seems to me the highest possible tribute by his enemies to the compelling importance of his contribution. Since what he has proposed evidently is seen to be unanswerable, the theology has been ignored, but the theologian has been assailed.

What is Rubenstein's message? It has been eloquently stated in various places. I believe the most cogent expression of his viewpoint on the centrality of the Holocaust is in his contribution to *Commentary*'s Symposium on Jewish Belief:

I believe the great single challenge to modern Judaism arises out of the question of God and the death camps. I am amazed at the silence of contemporary Jewish theologians on this most crucial and agonizing of all Jewish issues. How can Jews believe in an omnipotent, beneficient God after Auschwitz? Traditional Jewish theology maintains that God is the ultimate, omnipotent actor in the historical drama. It has interpreted every major catastrophe in Jewish history as God's punishment of a sinful Israel. I fail to see how this position can be maintained without regarding Hitler and the SS as instruments of God's will. The agony of European Jewry cannot be likened to the testing of Job. To see any purpose in the death camps, the traditional believer is forced to regard the most demonic, antihuman explosion in all history as a meaningful expression of God's purposes. The idea is simply too obscene for me to accept. I do not think that the full impact of Auschwitz has yet been felt in Jewish theology or Jewish life. Great religious revolutions have their own period of gestation. No man knows the hour when the full impact of Auschwitz will be felt, but no religious community can endure so hideous a wounding without undergoing vast inner disorders.

Though I believe that a void stands where once we experienced God's presence, I do not think Judaism has lost its meaning or its power. I do not believe that a theistic God is necessary for Jewish religious life. Dietrich Bonhoeffer has written that our problem is how to speak of God in an age of no religion. I believe that our problem is how to speak of religion in an age of no God. I have suggested that Judaism is the way in which we share the decisive times and crises of life through the traditions of our inherited community. The need for that sharing is not diminished in the time of the death of God. We not longer believe in the God who has the power to annul the tragic necessities of existence; the need religiously to share that existence remains.[8]

Rubenstein's is not an essentially destructive conclusion.

On the contrary, he draws from the Holocaust a constructive, if astringent, message:

> Death and rebirth are the great moments of religious experience. In the twentieth century the Jewish phoenix has known both: in Germany and eastern Europe, we Jews have tasted the bitterest and the most degrading of deaths. Yet death was not the last word. We do not pity ourselves. Death in Europe was followed by resurrection in our ancestral home. We are free as no men before us have ever been. Having lost everything, we have nothing further to lose and no further fear of loss. Our existence has in truth been a being-unto-death. We have passed beyond all illusion and hope. We have learned in the crisis that we were totally and nakedly alone, that we could expect neither support nor succor from God or from our fellow creatures. No men have known as we have how truly God in His holiness slays those to whom He gives life. This has been a liberating knowledge, at least for the survivors, and all Jews everywhere regard themselves as having escaped by the skin of their teeth, whether they were born in Europe or elsewhere. We have lost all hope and faith. We have also lost all possibility of disappointment. Expecting absolutely nothing from God or man, we rejoice in whatever we receive. We have learned the nakedness of every human pretense. No people has come to know as we have how deeply man is an insubstantial nothingness before the awesome and terrible majesty of the Lord. We accept our nothingness — nay, we even rejoice in it — for in finding our nothingness we have found both ourselves and the God who alone is true substance. We did not ask to be born; we did not ask for our absurd existence in the world; nor have we asked for the fated destiny which has hung about us as Jews. Yet we would not exchange it, nor would we deny it, for when nothing is asked for, nothing is hoped for, nothing is expected; all that we receive is truly grace.[9]

Fackenheim's contrary view is that "Auschwitz" produces a new commandment to the Jewish people: to preserve the

Jewish people and the Jewish religion. Michael Wyschogrod, in
"Faith and the Holocaust," summarizes Fackenheim's viewpoint as follows:

> What, then, is adequate?
>
> Only obedience to the Voice of Auschwitz. This
> voice, as heard by Fackenheim, commands the survival
> of Jews and Judaism. Because Hitler was bent upon the
> destruction of both, it is the duty of those Jews who
> survived Hitler to make sure that they do not do his
> work, that they do not, by assimilation, bring about the
> disappearance of what Hitler attempted but ultimately
> failed to destroy. For the religious Jew, this means that
> he must go on being religious, however inadequate
> Auschwitz has shown his frame of reference to be. And
> for the secular Jew, the Voice of Auschwitz commands
> not faith, which even the Voice of Auschwitz cannot
> command, but preservation of Jews and Judaism.
> Speaking of the significance of the Voice of Auschwitz
> for the secular Jew, Fackenheim writes: "No less
> inescapable is this Power for the secularist Jew who has
> all along been outside the Midrashic framework and this
> despite the fact that the Voice of Auschwitz does not
> enable him to return into this framework. He cannot
> return; but neither may he turn the Voice of Auschwitz
> against that of Sinai. For he may not cut off his secular
> present from the religious past: The Voice of Auschwitz
> commands Jewish unity." The sin of Rubenstein is,
> therefore, that he permits Auschwitz further to divide
> the Jewish people at a time when survival is paramount
> if Hitler is not to be handed a posthumous victory, and
> survival demands unity. Because this is so, Rubenstein
> should presumably soft-pedal his doubts so as not to
> threaten the Jewish people at a time when everything
> must be secondary to the issue of survival.[10]

What may be said in behalf of Fackenheim's argument?
Fackenheim has the merit of placing the Holocaust at the head
of Judaic theological discourse, and of doing so in such a way
that the central problem is *not* theodicy. Rubenstein's stress on
the issue of how a just God could have permitted so formidable

an injustice — an understatement of the issue to be sure — leads him to the position just now outlined. Fackenheim's formulation of the issue of the Holocaust in terms of its meaning to the secular, not to the religious, Jew sidesteps the surely insoluble issue of theology, and so opens a constructive and forward-looking discourse on the primary issue facing contemporary Judaism, the issue of secularity and disbelief.

Rubenstein tends to center his interest on the tragic events themselves, while Fackenheim prefers to make those events speak to the contemporary situation of Jewry. One may compare Rubenstein's mode of thought to that of the first-century apocalyptic visionaries, Fackenheim's to that of the rabbis of the same period. After 70 C.E. the issue of the destruction of the Second Temple predominated and could not be avoided. No religious discourse, indeed, no religious life, would then have been possible without attention to the meaning of that awesome event. The message of apocalypse was that the all-powerful God who had punished the people for their sins very soon would bring on the messianic age. People who heard this message fixed their gaze upon the future and eagerly awaited the messianic denouement. When confronted by the messianic claim of Bar Kokhba, they responded vigorously, undertaking a catastrophic and hopeless holy war.

The rabbis after 70 had a different message. It was not different from that of the apocalyptics in stressing the righteousness of God, who had punished the sin of Israel. But the conclusion drawn from that fact was *not* to focus attention on the future and on what would soon come to compensate for the catastrophe. The rabbis sought to devise a program for the survival and reconstruction of the saving remnant. The message was that just as God was faithful to punish sin, so he may be relied upon to respond to Israel's regeneration. The task of the hour therefore is to study Torah, carry out the commandments, and do deeds of loving-kindness. From the stubborn consideration of present and immediate difficulties therefore came a healthy and practical plan by which Israel might in truth hold on to what could be salvaged from disaster. Redemption will come. In the meanwhile there are things to do. Just as the Jews awaited a redemptive act of compassion from God, so they must now act compassionately in order to make themselves worthy of it. The tragedy thus produced two responses, the one obsessed with the disaster, the other concerned for what is to happen afterward, here and now.

It seems to me Rubenstein carries forward the messianic and apocalyptic, Fackenheim the rabbinical, mode of thinking. The difference between them is in perspective and focus, not in the contrast between a negative and destructive approach, on the one side, and an affirmative and constructive one, on the other. Rubenstein is not a nihilist; Fackenheim's "commanding Voice of Auschwitz" speaks to people beyond despair, demands commitment from the nihilist himself. In Fackenheim's behalf one must point to the remarkable pertinence of his message to the issues of the present. He has, in a way, transcended tragic events, just as did the first-century rabbis. Fackenheim does not say only the obvious, that one must believe despite disaster. He holds that the disaster itself is evidence in behalf of belief, a brilliant return to the rabbinic mode of response to catastrophe. In this regard, Rubenstein and Fackenheim, representative of the two extreme positions, cannot be reconciled, except within the events of which they speak. Confronting those events, both theologians perceive something "radically" new and without precedent in the history of Judaism. With that shared claim the two extremes come together.

Reform Judaism and Zionism: The Synthesis of American Judaism

Clearly, the two great messianic forces in modern Judaism, Reform Judaism and Zionism, seem to have shaped American Judaism. The vast majority of American Jews who are religious — who are Judaists — belong to Reform or Conservative synagogues. Nearly all American Jews, both religious and nonreligious, strongly support the State of Israel. It is, therefore, fair to ask how these two diverse movements have been shaped into a single conception of "Judaism," and have been merged by people who do not see themselves as Messianists at all, but who continue to live the timeless and unchanging life of the Diaspora.

How do American Jews conceive of "the good Jew"? That seems the fair way to formulate the question, What is the state of Judaism in modernity? Truly, it is in ordinary, everyday life that we discern the meaning of religion. There we discover the practical result of reflections on time and eternity, God and humankind, which form the focus of the religious experience. Accordingly, we cannot conclude our analysis of modern and contemporary Judaism without attending to the practical outcome of the past two centuries of change and upheaval.

In 1967, the great sociologist of Judaism, Marshall Sklare, with Joseph Greenblum, published an account of the meaning of Jewishness among middle class, suburban Jews, *Jewish Identity on the Suburban Frontier* (New York: Basic Books, 1967). There, Sklare and Greenblum describe the components of the conception of the "good Jew." In interviewing Jews of Lakeville (the name of the suburb was fictionalized), Sklare wisely did not ask about abstract beliefs or practices. He simply inquired, "In your opinion, for a Jew to be considered a good Jew, which of the following must he do? Which are desirable but not essential that he do?" In other words, what does a person do because he or she is Jewish and a Judaist? Here are the items that received the highest ranking:

Lead an ethical and moral life	93%
Accept being a Jew and not try to hide it	85%
Support all humanitarian causes	67%
Promote civic betterment	67%
Gain respect of Christian neighbors	59%
Help the underprivileged improve their lot	58%
Know the fundamentals of Judaism	48%
Work for equality of Negroes	44%

On this result, Sklare comments, "At first glance the ideal of Jewishness ... seems to be that of the practice of good citizenship and an upright life. To be a good Jew means to be an ethical individual; it also means to be kind, helpful, and interested in the welfare of neighbors, fellow Americans, and of humanity at large. But further examination leads to the conclusion that Lakeville's ideal of Jewishness is more than a sophisticated version of the Boy Scout who guides the frail old lady across a busy street. It is more than the practice of ethics. There is, for example, the aspect of Jewish self-acceptance; our respondents feel that in order to be a good Jew, it is essential freely and proudly to acknowledge one's identity. Does this attitude, we wonder, result from the belief that Jewish existence is a great and wonderful mystery as well as a distinction and obligation which Gentiles are the poorer for not sharing? . . ."

When we look back upon the great forces of modern Judaism, Zionism and Reform, we must wonder what effect, if any, they have had upon ordinary folk. For the Lakeville study reveals hardly any Zionist impact at all upon the values of the community. True, other parts of Sklare's study reveal that the population of the Jewish community is "for Israel," meaning that it wants to help the State of Israel survive and prosper. But one hardly has to share the Zionist analysis of Jewish history and of the Jewish condition to adopt such a positive, if very distant, approach. The full meaning and weight of anti-Semitism as interpreted by Zionism need have no meaning at all for people to conclude they should give money to the State of Israel. On the contrary, the pro-Israeli actions and attitudes taken to be normative of American Jews are virtually unrelated to the basic theses of Zionism. They are a passive response to facts created by Zionism, rather than an active participation in the formation of a Zionist conception and policy for American Judaism. Zionism as a viewpoint, as a messianic force, is dead in Sklare's Lakeville study.

What of Reform Judaism? In general, Sklare observes, "The acts which the good Jew is obliged to perform include advancing the general welfare, promoting social reform, and increasing intergroup amity." In our discussion of Reform Judaism, we find valid precedents for this emphasis upon social ethics. But in Lakeville there is hardly a hint that "being a decent human being" is part of that "messianic Judaism" of which the classical Reformers wrote. On the contrary, one does not have to be a Reform Jew, a Rabbinic Jew, or even Jewish at all, to agree with these prescriptions. Contrast the religious attitude permeating the ethical teaching of Joel, son of Abraham Shemariah, whose words we read at the close of the last chapter. He too counsels his children to seek peace with everyone and contend with no one ("support all humanitarian causes"), and to forego rights, envy no one ("lead an ethical and moral life"), and to be at peace with all the world, with Jew and Gentile ("gain respect of Christian neighbors"). Curiously, Joel

would hardly have reason to differ with the Lakeville Jews.
What they believe is what he taught his heirs. The difference is
that for Joel, it was the teaching of Habakkuk, the message of
Torah, which was to be expressed through ethical action: "The
righteous shall live by his faith." The right living goes on in
Lakeville, but with slight attention to faith.

In this regard, Sklare lists the "desirable" things Jews in
Lakeville feel they should do:

Be well versed in Jewish history and culture	73%
Marry within the Jewish faith	51%
Contribute to Jewish philanthropies	49%
Belong to Jewish organizations	49%
Know the fundamentals of Judaism	48%
Support Israel	47%
Attend weekly services	46%
Attend services on high holy days	46%
Belong to a synagogue	44%

While all these actions indicate the will of the Jewish community to continue as a distinctive group, only a few of them
bear any relationship to religion as it is commonly practiced, for
example, belief and worship. Knowledge of "Jewish history and
culture" cannot be assumed to be equivalent to study of Torah.
As Sklare comments, "The Lakeville Jew remains considerably
more Jewish in action than in thought."

In other words, it is difficult to discover, in the actual
opinions and actions of ordinary American Jews, either Zionism
or Reform Judaism — or, quite obviously, any other formulation or expression of Judaism. That classical Rabbinic Judaism
is absent in Lakeville may be taken for granted. In this regard,
we recall the speech of Jacob David Wilowsky, a great rabbinic
authority in Russia, in 1900. As cited by Sklare, he told an
audience in New York City, "Any Jew who comes to American
is a sinner. . . ." Judaism has no chance of survival on American
soil: "It was not only home that the Jews left behind in Europe.
It was their Torah, their Talmud, their yeshivot, their entire
Jewish way of life." That, to be sure, is not the whole story of
what happened with modern, American Judaism. But, as we see
clearly in the Lakeville example, it surely is a significant part.

To put matters very simply: Zionism and Reform Judaism,

the two most consequential forces in the modern age of Judaism, cannot be said to have shaped the values, the mythic perceptions, the goals, or even the life-story, of the American Jews ("Lakeville") under study. On the contrary, neither the messianism that led to the creation of the State of Israel nor the messianism that led to the formation of Reform Judaism as a positive, hopeful, radical reconception of Judaism has left a perceptible mark upon the mind of American Jewry. Why do we say so? Because the things which one must do because he or she is a Zionist, on the one side, or because he or she is a Reform Jew, on the other, hardly seem very important in Lakeville. And this is because the things that the Lakeville Jews say one must do because he or she is Jewish have not been selected on account of the larger messianic aspiration of Reform Judaism, even though in some ways these indeed are the effects of that aspiration. If the Lakeville Jews say the most important thing is to lead an ethical and moral life, the reason clearly is not that, in so doing, one will bring nearer the messianic age. So the effects of Zionism continue in the pro-Israeli attitudes of the Lakeville Jews, just as the effects of Reform Judaism continue in the emphasis upon ethics characteristic of the community. But Zionism and Reform Judaism as encompassing conceptions of the world have not generated, and do not stand behind, the stated attitudes. At best, Zionism and Reform Judaism acquired a momentum of their own long ago and show up, therefore, in the profile of Lakeville's Judaism. But Zionism and Reform Judaism do not seem to speak to today's Jews of Lakeville.

Let us now turn from a concrete case to the much larger setting of world Judaism. What we shall see is that Lakeville is a microcosm. In fact, what has *not* happened in Lakeville — the continuing capacity of the modern Messianism to speak to the modern Jew — also has *not* happened anywhere else. Both movements have run out of steam, have lost their motive force.

Torah and Messiah

Modern Jews have in common a yearning for the climax and conclusion of history. This is the mark of modernity: the sense that humanity has passed through a long dark age and has come to the final period in the history of humankind. Reform Judaism spoke confidently of inaugurating a messianic age. Zionism, likewise, proposed the final solution to the Jewish problem, resorting to the messianic language imbedded in the rabbinic tradition. What the two modern movements in contemporary Judaism have in common is the capacity to take seriously what happens in the world. Rabbinic Judaism, we already know, stresses the importance of continuity amidst change.

If, now, we review in our minds what we learned about the time during which Rabbinic Judaism took shape, we see a remarkable fact. The twentieth century is strikingly similar to the first century. Both centuries are marked by a tension between change and changelessness, and, of far greater significance, both centuries are marked by disaster. The destruction of the Temple of Jerusalem in the year 70 swept away the foundations of the Judaic conception of the world. The destruction of European Jewry, an event of immensely great weight in social terms, bears a curious resemblance, in its impact upon the mind and imagination of the Jewish people, to the destruction of the Second Temple. The messianic optimism of Reform Judaism ceased to be persuasive with the Holocaust. But the other Messianism, that is, Zionism, was able to cope with that event.

Nineteen sixty-seven seemed the climactic moment in the messianic history written by Zionism, the point at which the history of the Jewish people appeared truly and finally to have ended in its former mold and shape. The new history, the history of Zion redeemed, seemed to begin. With the State of Israel's military victory and the return to the old Temple site, which had been closed off to Jewish access for many decades, the final meaning of the modern age appeared to have been revealed. So far as "the coming of the Messiah" or the messianic view stresses a radical and complete change in the mode of being of the Jewish people, 1967 marks the end of the history begun in the year 70, confirms the theory of redemption following disaster and hope following despair, that had long constituted the view of reality by which Rabbinic Judaism interpreted the life of the Jewish people.

But the messianic hope for a climax and conclusion proved

a fantasy. Six years later, the war of 1973 made it clear that history simply did not end in 1967. The precarious, desperate situation of Israel, the Jewish people, continues as before. A new event emphasized the chanciness, the desperation of the Jewish condition, which had characterized the twenty centuries before. The State of Israel solved many problems, to be sure, but it did not and does not constitute the fulfillment of the messianic hope.

This indeed is the human condition, the experience of continuity when one yearns for completion, of going on and on, fatigued through time, with no end in sight. It is the experience of humankind which sees the sun rise, the sun set, the world continue, which experiences birth and death and asks, "How long?" With its reentry into an unredeemed world, Zionism confronted the condition of insecurity characteristic of former times. The myth of redemption no longer conformed to the perceived reality of everyday life. Messianism confronted the sense that important questions affecting one's own life and destiny are often in the hands of others. This is the experience of human frailty and weakness, of the human condition which ought to have ended with the messianic realization, but which did not end.

Modern men and women and modern Jews among them sought to bring an end to the human condition of suffering and death. Through science and technology they alleviated the situation of humankind but they named it redemption; they wished to call it the messianic age. They found provisional solutions to enduring, permanent problems, and looked forward to the imminent end and climax of history. Just as the wars and revolutions produced the dehumanization of much of human-kind, and the end of the democratic hope called into question the optimism and sense of self-reliance and self-command of the nineteenth century, so for the Jews the disasters of the two World Wars placed in jeopardy the hopes of the nineteenth century optimists, Messianists, whether Reform or Zionists. Their hopes diminished for a radical change in the Jewish condition, which corresponded to the radical change in the social and economic and political circumstances of the Jewish people.

The Messianism of first century Judaism collapsed with the destruction of the Second Temple. What emerged in the next fifty years from about 70 to about 120 was the alternative, Rabbinic Judaism. It was in the setting and context of failed Messianism that Rabbinic Judaism took shape. Contemporary Jews find themselves, wherever they live, in the setting and context of today's failed Messianisms. Perhaps, therefore, the perspective of Rabbinic Judaism may prove pertinent. What was and is that perspective upon history?

We know the answer from the prayers we have read. First, Jews hope for the coming of the Messiah, but, second, until that time they do their duty. In this connection we consider the message of one of the founders of Rabbinic Judaism, Yohanan ben Zakkai: "If you are out in the field and planting a sapling and someone comes and says to you, 'The Messiah has come,' what should you do? First, plant the sapling, and then go forth and receive him." The central issue of Rabbinic Judaism is the location of meaning and significance in the ordinary, undramatic, unhistorical days before the coming of the Messiah or the messianic age. The answer of Rabbinic Judaism is to discover, in ordinary everyday events, meanings of cosmic significance. This we saw in the nurture and application of a great myth, the myth of Moses, "our rabbi," and the dual Torah, living revelation, to the learning and doing of the revealed traditions of old. This conception of Torah opened the affairs of the home and street to revelation in the here and now. It gave ordinary people living ordinary lives the confidence that what they do matters now and not solely in some distant future or in some never-never land. Common folk gained the sense that it is specifically the things they do control that matter and have cosmic significance. Rabbinic Judaism represents the turning away from grand historical events and the turning toward the simple and concrete things people can control, things history does not take seriously — what I eat for breakfast, how I behave toward my neighbor. It is the genius of Rabbinic Judaism to link these humble and everyday matters to the larger themes of history and Messianism: "Plant the tree, but then receive him." Rabbinic Judaism bridges the gap between the great public affairs of nations and the private and simple doings of ordinary people.

Why was that important and why can that approach become important once again? Because, until history ends, life does go onward through time. Things do happen. If people are fortunate, they will live benign, commonplace lives. But then they also have a yearning for larger meaning. It is natural to ask, How long? In linking the cosmic and world-historical realm with the home and the hearth, Rabbinic Judaism sought and seeks to endow with meaning that interim between the beginning and the end, between one disaster and another, which people know as life.

The real dilemma of modern men and women, living in an age in which the human condition for many no longer includes the sheer struggle for survival — for food, shelter, clothing — is dealing with the banality and commonplaceness of life. How to overcome the boredom of prosperity, the triviality and absence of larger meaning characterizing people for whom life consists of the undifferentiated passage of time, the sameness of daily work in unimportant jobs? For some, escape into faddism lends a trace of color to otherwise drab existence. For others, adventure or experiment suffices. But for the many too dull to dream, too worn down to do, and yet, despite it all, too human to find life's meaning only in ultimate death, what is left? It is clear that Rabbinic Judaism came into being to deal with that circumstance, of a life too commonplace to be deemed tragic, yet too urgent to be ignored. Curiously, it was in the crucible of ultimate disaster, in the storm and turbulence of weighty events, that Rabbinic Judaism was born. And in the face of catastrophe, Rabbinic Judaism spoke of what to do when catastrophe was done. The interim between beginning and end, between one world-historical cataclysm and the next, between birth and lonely death — that is the setting for the quiet drama of the ancient rabbis' Torah.

Notes

1. Quoted from Louis Ginzberg, "Israel Salanter," in Jacob Neusner, ed., *Understanding Rabbinic Judaism*, (New York: Ktav Publishing House, 1974), pp. 372-373.
2. Quoted in Joseph L. Blau, ed., *Reform Judaism, A Historical Perspective*, (New York: Ktav Publishing House, 1973), pp. 102-103.
3. Quoted in Abraham J. Feldman, *Reform Judaism, A Guide for Reform Jews*, (New York: Behrman House, 1956), pp. 7-8.

4. Quoted in Arthur Hertzberg, *The Zionist Idea* (New York: Herzl Press, 1959), pp. 215-216.

5. Ibid., pp. 218-219.

6. Ibid., pp. 17-18.

7. Ibid., pp. 266-267.

8. Quoted in Richard L. Rubenstein, *After Auschwitz*, (Indianapolis: The Bobbs-Merrill Co., Inc., 1966), pp. 153-154.

9. Ibid., pp. 128-129.

10. Quoted from Michael Wyschograd, "Faith and the Holocaust," in *Judaism*, Summer 1971, pp. 286-294.

Glossary

Aaron: The brother of Moses. The Pentateuch represents him as the founder of the priesthood. It is believed that a Messiah will come from among his descendants.

Adon Olam: "Lord of the World" hymn containing dogmas of devine unity, timelessness, and providence.

Aggadah: Lit.: Telling, narration. Generally: Lore, theology, fable, biblical exegesis, ethics.

Ahavah: Love; *Ahavah rabbah*, great love; first words of prayer preceding *Shema.*

Akabya: Akabya ben Mehallel, an early first century authority to whom is attributed the saying (*Mishnah Avot* 3:1), "Consider three things and you will not fall into the hands of transgression. Know whence you are come, and whither you are going, and before whom you are going to give account and reckoning."

Alenu: "It is incumbent upon us."

Aliyah: Going up; migration to the Land of Israel.

Am HaAres: Lit.: People of the land. Rabbinic usage: boor, unlearned, not a disciple of the sage.

Amidah: Lit.: Standing. The main section of obligatory prayers for morning, afternoon, and evening, containing eighteen benedictions: 1. God of the fathers; 2. praise of God's power; 3. holiness; 4. prayer for knowledge; 5. prayer for

177

repentence; 6. prayer for forgiveness; 7. prayer for redemption; 8. prayer for healing the sick; 9. blessing of agricultural produce; 10. prayer for ingathering of dispersed Israel; 11. prayer for righteous judgment; 12. prayer for punishment of the wicked and heretics; 13. prayer for reward of the pious; 14. prayer for rebuilding Jerusalem; 15. prayer for restoration of the house of David; 16. prayer for acceptance of prayers; 10. prayer of thanks; 18. prayer for restoration of Temple service; 19. prayer for peace.

Amora: Rabbinical teacher in Palestine and Babylonia in talmudic times (ca. 200-500 C.E.). Plural: *Amoraim.*

Apikoros: Hebrew for Epicurus. Generally: Belief in hedonism.

Ashkenaz(im): European Jews, those who follow the customs originating in medieval German Judaism.

Ashre: "Happy are they": Psalm 145, read in morning and afternoon worship.

Av, Ninth of: Day of Mourning for destruction of Jerusalem Temple in 586 B.C.E. and 70 C.E.

Baal Shem Tov (ca. 1700-1760): Master of the Good Name, founder of Hasidism.

Baruch: The secretary of the biblical prophet, Jeremiah, was Baruch b. Neriah. An anonymous writer, at the time of the destruction of the Second Temple in 70 C.E., took Baruch's name and claimed to write his vision at the time of the destruction of the First Temple. He meant to comfort the people of his own day by giving them the message written by the scribe at the time of the first destruction.

Bar Mitzvah: Ceremony at which a thirteen-year-old boy becomes an adult member of the Jewish community; an adult male Jew who is obligated to carry out the commandments (*mitzvah; mitzvot*).

Bat Mitzvah: Adult female Jew who is obligated to carry out commandments; marked by ceremony as for *Bar Mitzvah.*

B.C.E.: Before the Common Era; used in place of B.C.

Berakhah: Blessing or praise.

Bet Am: House of people; early word for synagogue.

Bet Din: Court of law judging civil, criminal, and religious cases according to *halakhah.*

Bet Midrash: House of study.

Bimah: Area in synagogue from which worship is led.

Birkat HaMazon: Grace after meals.

Brit milah: Covenant of circumcision; removal of foreskin of penis on eighth day after birth.

C.E.: Common Era; used instead of A.D.

Central Conference of American Rabbis: Association of Reform rabbis.

Cohen/kohen: Priest.

Conservative Judaism: Religious movement, reacting against early Reform; attempts to adapt Jewish law to modern life on the basis of principles of change inherent in traditional laws.

Dayyan: Judge in Jewish court.

Dead Sea Community: See Essenes.

Decalogue: Ten Words, the Ten Commandments; Hebrew = *'Aseret HaDibrot.*

Derekh Eretz: Lit.: The way of the land; normal custom, correct conduct; good manners, etiquette.

Diaspora: Dispersion, exile of Jews from the Land of Israel.

Dietary laws: Pertaining to animal food. Pious Jews may eat only fish that have fins and scales, and animals with parted hooves who chew the cud (for example, sheep or cows, but not camels or pigs). Animals must be ritually slaughtered (Hebrew: *shehitah*), a humane method of slaughter accompanied by blessing of thanks. Jews may not eat shellfish, worms, snails, flesh torn from a living animal, and so forth. Any mixture of meat and milk is forbidden; after eating meat, one may not eat dairy products for from one to six hours, depending on custom. Fish are neutral *(pareve). See kosher.*

El, Elohim: God, divinity.

Erev: Evening, sunset, beginning of a holy day.

Eschatological: An adjective, based upon the noun *eschaton,* the end of time. Eschatological then means things pertaining to the end of time and the coming of the Messiah.

Essenes: Sect that flourished during the last two centuries before the destruction of the Second Temple in 70 C.E. The Essenes, as described by Josephus, set up communes near the Dead Sea. It is likely that the books discovered near the Dead Sea ("Dead Sea Scrolls") derive from a group of Essenes, or people much like the Essenes.

Etrog: Citron, one of four species carried in the synagogue on *Sukkot,* from Leviticus 23:40, "fruit of a goodly tree."

Exilarch: Head of the exile; Aramaic: *Resh Galuta;* head of the Jewish community in Babylonia in talmudic and medieval times.

Ezra: A scribe who lived in the fifth century B.C.E. and whose life and writings are contained in the Book of Ezra. He led the people who rebuilt the Temple after its first destruction. At about the time of the destruction, his name was adopted by various anonymous writers, who addressed the problems of their own time with the message relevant to his. Like the writer(s) who took the name of Baruch, their idea was that, since Ezra had been a leading figure in the beginnings of the Second Temple, he would be listened to in the time of its destruction. The various apocryphal books in the name of Ezra are divided into parts. Here we cite Second Ezra.

Gaon: Eminence, excellency, title of the head of Babylonian academies; later, distinguished talmudic scholar.

Gedaliah, Fast of: Third day of the autumn month of Tishri, commemorating the assassination of Gedaliah (2 Kings 25, Jer. 40:1).

Geiger, Abraham (1810-1874): Early reformer in Germany. He produced a modern prayer book, wanted Judaism to become a world religion.

Gemara: Completion; comments and discussions of Mishnah. Mishnah + Gemara = Talmud.

Get: Bill of divorce, required to dissolve a Jewish marriage.

Golus: Ashkenazic pronunciation of *galut*, exile; life in *Diaspora;* discrimination, humiliation.

Halakhah: "The way things are done," from *halakh:* go; more broadly, the prescriptive, legal tradition.

Hanukkah: Festival of lights, which comes in December, commemorating the victory of the Maccabees, Jewish leaders in the second century B.C.E., over the Hellenistic party among the Jews supported by the Greek empire of the Seleucids. The Hellenizers had taken over the Temple and made it "unclean"; the Maccabees recaptured the Temple and "purified" it. They were able to locate only a small amount of oil for the holy lamp, but the oil lasted for eight days, until a new supply was obtained. Accordingly, for eight days, candles are kindled in commemoration of the miracle.

Haskalah: Jewish Enlightenment, the eighteenth-century movement of rationalists.

Hebrew Union College — Jewish Institute of Religion: Founded in Cincinnati in 1875, the center for training Reform rabbis and teachers; campuses in Los Angeles, Cincinnati, New York City, and Jerusalem.

Heder: Room; elementary school for early education.

Herod: Jewish king, ally of Rome, who ruled from ca. 40-10 B.C.E. He was a powerful and important king. Through his alliance with Rome he secured influence beyond the Jewish community of Palestine. He put an end to the sectarian and partisan bickering of the period of the last of the Maccabees and, in consequence, some political sects were suppressed.

Hiddush: Novella; new point, insight, given as a comment on classical text. Often ingenious; sometimes hair splitting.

Hillel: First-century Pharisaic leader, taught "Do not unto others what you would not have them do unto you."

Hillul HaShem: Profanation of God's name; doing something to bring disrepute on Jews or Judaism, particularly among non-Jews.

Hillul Shabbat: Profanation of the Sabbath.

Hol HaMoed: Intermediate days of festivals of Passover, *Sukkot.*

Huppah: Canopy under which marriage ceremony takes place.

Jehovah: Transliteration of Divine name, based on misunderstanding of Hebrew letters *YHWH*. Jews do not pronounce name of God; they refer to the name as *Adonai*, Lord. Translators took vowels of Adonai and added them to consonants *JHVH*, hence JeHoVah.

Jewish Theological Seminary: Founded 1888; center for training Conservative rabbis and teachers; campuses in New York City, Los Angeles, and Jerusalem.

Josephus: A Jewish general who led an army in the war against Rome, which began in 66 C.E. He later surrendered and, after the war, wrote the *History of the War* and also a *History of the Jews.* His works are a primary source for the study of Jewish history and of Judaism before 70.

Joshua ben Hananiah: A leading rabbi in the period after 70 C.E., Joshua was a disciple of Yohanan ben Zakkai.

Judah the Patriarch: Head of Palestinian Jewish community, 200 C.E.; promulgator of Mishnah.

Kabbalah: Lit.: Tradition; later, the mystical Jewish tradition.

Kaddish: Doxology at the end of principal sections of Jewish service; praise of God with congregational response, "May his great name be praised eternally." Eschatological emphasis: Hope for speedy advent of Messiah. Also recited by mourners.

Karaites: Eighth- to twelfth-century Middle Eastern Jewish sect, rejected oral Torah, lived by written one alone.

Kehillah: Jewish community.

Keneset Israel: Assembly of Israel; Jewish people as a whole.

Keriat Shema: Recital of *Shema.*

Ketuvah: Marriage contract specifying obligations of groom to bride.

Ketuvim: Writings; biblical books of Psalms, Proverbs, Job, Song of Songs, Ruth, Lamentations, Ecclesiastes, Esther, Daniel, Ezra, Nehemiah, and Chronicles.

Kibbutz: Israeli collective settlement.

Kibbutz galuyyot: Gathering of the exiles; eschatological hope that all Israel will be restored to the land; now applied to migration of Jewish communities to state of Israel.

Kiddush: Sanctification, generally of wine, in proclamation of Sabbath or a festival.

Kiddush HaShem: Sanctification of the name of God; applies to conduct of Jews among non-Jews which brings esteem on Jews, Judaism; in medieval times: Martyrdom.

Kol Nidre: All vows; prayer opening *Yom Kippur* eve service, declaring that all vows made rashly during the year and not carried out are null and void.

Kosher: Lit.: Fit, proper; applies to anything suitable for use according to Jewish law.

Lag BeOmer: Thirty-third day in seven-week period of counting the *Omer*, from second day of Passover to Pentecost (Lev. 23:15); day of celebration for scholars.

Lamed Vav: Thirty-six unrecognized men of humble vocation by whose merit the world exists; they bring salvation in crisis.

Lulav: Palm branch used on *Sukkot.* (See drawing, page 183.)

Maariv: Evening service.

ETROG (CITRUS FRUIT) AND
LULAV (PALM BRANCH) FOR SUKKOT

Maccabees: Leaders of a revolt against the Syrian-Greek rulers of Palestine in the first third of the second century B.C.E.; the Maccabees eventually achieved independence. From ca. 140-40, their dynasty ruled Jewish Palestine. In their time, a number of political-religious sects or philosophical groups formed, including Pharisees, Sadducees, and Essenes.

Magen David: Shield of David, six-pointed star; distinctive Jewish symbol after the seventeenth century.

Mah Nishtannah: "Wherein is this night different from all others?"; opening words of four questions asked by child at Passover *seder.*

Mahzor: Prayer book for New Year and Day of Atonement.

Malkuyyot: Sovereignties, section of New Year Additional Service devoted to theme of God's sovereignty.

Maoz Tsur: "Fortress, Rock of My Salvation"; Hanukkah hymn.

Maror: Bitter herbs, consumed at Passover *seder* in remembrance of bitter life of Hebrew slaves in Egypt.

Mashgiah: Supervisor of rituals, particularly ritual slaughter; must be expert in laws, pious and God-fearing. An ignorant man, motivated by financial gain, cannot supervise religious rites.

Maskil: Enlightened man, follower of *Haskalah* = Enlightenment.

Masorah: Tradition.

Matzah: Unleavened bread, used for *Passover.*

Mazzal: Lit.: Constellation, star.

Mazzal tov: Good luck.

Megillah: Scroll; usually: Scroll of Esther, read at *Purim.*

Melavveh Malkah: Accompanying the Queen; meal held at the end of the holy day to prolong Sabbath celebration.

Menorah: Candelabrum; nine-branched *menorah* is used at *Hanukkah;* seven-branched *menorah* was used in ancient Temple.

Messiah: Eschatological king to rule at end of time.

Mezuzah: Parchment containing first two paragraphs of *Shema,* rolled tightly and placed in case, attached to doorposts of home.

Midrash: Exegesis of Scripture; also applied to collection of such exegeses.

Mikveh: Ritual bath for immersion to wash away impurity; baptism.

Minhah: Afternoon prayers.

Minyan: Quorum needed for worship: Ten.

Mishnah: Code of law promulgated by Judah the Prince (ca. 200 C.B.); in six parts, it concerns agricultural laws; festival and Sabbath law; family and personal status; torts, damages, and civil law; laws pertaining to the sanctuary; and laws of ritual cleanness.

Mitnaged: Opponent; opposition to Hasidism by rationalists and talmudists.

Mitzvah: Commandments; technical sense: Scriptural or rabbinical injunctions; later, also used in sense of good deed; every human activity may represent an act of obedience to divine will.

Moed: Festival.

Mohel: Ritual circumciser.

Musaf: Additional service on Sabbath and festivals, commemorating additional offering in Temple times.

Musar: Lit.: Chastisement; instruction in right behavior; movement in modern Judaism emphasizing study and practice of ethical traditions, founded by Israel Salanter (1810-1883).

Nasi: Prince.

Navi: Prophet.

Neder: Vow.

Neilah: Closing service at end of *Yom Kippur*, at nightfall when fast ends.

Niggun: Melody, traditional tune for prayer.

Olam Hazeh, Olam Haba: This world, the world to come.

Omer: Sheaf cut in barley harvest.

Oneg Shabbat: Sabbath delight.

Orthodoxy: Traditional Judaism; belief in historical event of revelation at Sinai of oral and written Torah, in binding character of Torah, and in authority of Torah-sages to interpret Torah.

Passover: Hebrew: *Pesah*, festival commemorating exodus from Egypt, in spring month of Nisan (April).

Peot: Corners, Leviticus 19:27 forbids removing hair at corners of head, thus Orthodox Jews do not cut earlocks.

Peshat: Literal meaning of Scripture, distinct from *derash*, or homily.

Pharisee: from Hebrew, *Parush*, separatist; party in ancient Judaism teaching oral Torah revealed at Sinai along with written, preserved among prophets and sages down to the Pharisaic party; Pharisees espoused prophetic ideals and translated them through legislation to everyday life of Jewry. Distinctive beliefs: 1. immortality of the soul; 2. existence of angels; 3. divine providence; 4. freedom of will; 5. resurrection of the dead; 6. oral Torah.

Pilpul: Dialectical reasoning in study of oral law.

Piyyut: Synagogue poetry.

Pseudepigraph: A writer who signs his book with another's name, for example, with the name of a famous ancient authority, in order to gain greater credence and authority. *Pseudepigraphica:* Books written by people who sign other peoples' names. The names that were selected — Adam, Enoch, Ezra, Baruch — were of people in olden times who were supposed to have foreknowledge of the end of days.

Purim: Festival commemorating deliverance of Persian Jews from extermination in fifth century B.C.E., as related in Scroll of Esther; occurs on 14th of Adar, generally in March.

Qumran: A place near the Dead Sea at which some of the Dead Sea Scrolls were first discovered in 1947.

Rava: Fourth-century talmudic master, head of Babylonian school at Mahoza.

Rabbi: My master, title for teacher of Oral Torah.

Rabbinical Assembly: Association of Conservative rabbis.

Rabbinical Council: Association of Orthodox rabbis in United States.

Rashi: A name for R. Solomon Isaac (1040-1105), composed of RAbbi SHlomo Yizhak, *RSHY*, hence, Rashi. He was the writer of the most widely consulted of all commentaries on the Bible and Talmud.

Reconstructionism: Movement to develop modern, naturalist theology for Judaism; founded by Mordecai M. Kaplan (b. 1881); emphasizes Jewish peoplehood, sees Judaism as natural outgrowth of Jewish people's efforts to insure survival and answer basic human questions.

Reform: Religious movement advocating change of tradition to conform to conditions of modern life. Holds *halakhah* to be human creation, subject to judgment of humankind; sees Judaism as historical religious experience of Jewish people.

Rosh Hashanah: New Year, first day of Tishri (September).

Rosh Yeshivah: Head of talmudical academy.

Sabbateanism: Movement of followers of *Shabbetai Zevi* (*q.v.*) (1626-1676), Messianic leader who became an apostate. Followers believed his apostasy was part of divine plan.

Sadducees: Sect of Temple priests and sympathizers; stressed written Torah and the right of the priesthood to interpret it against Pharisaic claim that oral tradition held by Pharisees was valid; rejected belief in resurrection of the dead, immortality of soul, angels, divine providence.

Sanhedrin: Jewish legislative-administrative agency in Temple times.

Seder: Order; Passover home service.

Sefer Torah: Scroll of Torah.

Selihot: Penitential prayers, recited before New Year.

Semikhah: Laying on of hands; ordination.

Sephardi(m): Descendants of Spanish Jewry, generally in Mediterranean countries.

Shabbetai Zevi (1626-1676): Kabbalist who made mystical revelations, he announced himself as Messiah in Smyrna

(Turkey) synagogue, 1665, went to Constantinople to claim his kingdom from sultan, was imprisoned, and converted to Islam.

Shaharit: Morning service; dawn.

Shalom: Peace. Traditional Hebrew greeting.

Shammai: Colleague of Hillel, first century Pharisaic sage.

Shavuot: Feast of weeks; Pentecost; commemorates giving of Torah at Mt. Sinai.

Shehitah: Ritual slaughter; consists of cutting through both windpipe and gullet by means of sharp knife, examining to see both have been cut through.

Shekhinah: Presence of God in world.

Shema: Proclamation of unity of God: Deuteronomy 6:4-9, 11:13-21, Numbers 15:37-41.

Shemini Atzeret: Eighth day of solemn assembly (Num. 30:35); last day of *Sukkot.* This is a holy day in itself.

Sheva Berakhot: Seven Blessings recited at wedding ceremony.

Shiva: Seven days of mourning following burial of close relative.

Shohet: Ritual slaughterer.

Shofar: Ram's horn, sounded during high holy day period, from a month before New Year until end of Yom Kippur.

Shoferot: Shofar-verses, concerning revelation, read in New Year Additional Service.

Shulhan Arukh: Prepared table; code of Jewish law by Joseph Karo, published 1565; authoritative for Orthodox Jewry.

Siddur: Jewish prayer book for all days except holy days.

Simhah: Celebration.

Simhat Torah: Rejoicing of law; second day of *Shemini Atzeret,* on which the Torah-reading cycle is completed; celebrated with song and dance.

Sukkah: Booth, tabernacle. (See drawing, page 188.)

Sukkot: Autumn harvest festival, ending high holy day season.

Synagogue: Greek translation of Hebrew *bet hakeneset,* house of assembly. Place of Jewish prayer, study, assembly.

Takkanah: Decree, ordinance issued by rabbinical authority.

Tallit: Prayer shawl, four-cornered cloth with fringes (Num. 15:38) worn by adult males during morning service.

Talmid Hakham: Disciple of the wise.

Talmud: Mishnah (q.v.) plus commentary on the Mishnah produced in rabbinical academies from ca. 200-500 C.E. (called *Gemara*) from the Talmud. Two Talmuds were

A SUKKAH

produced, one in Palestine, the other in Babylonia. From 500 C.E. onward, Babylonian Talmud was the primary source for Judaic law and theology.

Talmud Torah: Study of Torah; education.

Tanakh: Hebrew Bible; formed of *Torah, Nevi'im, Ketuvim,* or *Pentateuch, Prophets, Writings,* hence *TaNaKh.*

Tanna: One who studies and teaches; a rabbinical master mentioned in *Mishnah* is called a *tanna.*

Tehillim: Psalms.

Tefillin: Phylacteries worn by adult males during morning service, based on Exodus 13:1, 11, Deuteronomy 6:4-9, 11:13-21. These passages are written on parchment, placed in leather cases, and worn on left arm and forehead.

Tekiah: Sounding of *shofar* on New Year.

Teref, terefa: Lit.: Torn; generally: Unkosher food.

Torah: Lit.: Revelation. At first, the Five Books of Moses; then Scriptures as a whole; then the whole corpus of revelation, both written and oral, taught by Pharisaic Judaism. *Talmud*

Torah: Study of Torah. Standing by itself, Torah can mean "study," the act of learning and discussion of the tradition.

Tosafot: Comments on the *Talmud*, additions generally to the commentary of *Rashi*. The *Tosafists*, authorities who produced *Tosafot*, flourished during the twelfth and thirteenth centuries in Northern France.

Tosefta: Supplements to the *Mishnah*.

Tzaddik: Righteous man; among Hasidism, intermediary, master of hasidic circle.

Tzedakah: Righteousness; used for charity, philanthropy.

Tzidduk HaDin: Justification of the judgment; prayer of dying Jew.

Tzitzit: Fringes of *tallit*.

Wissenschaft des Judentums: Science of Judaism; scientific study using scholarly methods of history and philosophy for study of Jewish religion, literature, and history; founded in nineteenth-century Germany.

Yahrzeit: Anniversary of death of relative.

Yahveh: See Jehovah.

Yamim Noraim: Days of Awe: *Rosh Hashanah*, intervening days, and *Yom Kippur*, ten in all.

Yavneh: A town near the southern coast of Palestine ("the Land of Israel") where, after the destruction of the Temple in 70, important survivors came together.

Yeshiva: Session; talmudic academy.

Yetzer HaRa, Yetzer Tov: Evil inclination, good inclination.

Yiddish: Jewish language of Eastern Europe, now used in the United States, Israel, Argentina, Canada, and Mexico, in addition to vernacular; originally a Judeo-German dialect, with large number of Hebrew and Slavic words.

Yom Kippur: Day of Atonement, fast day for penitence.

Zealots: Jews who believed that the end of time was at hand at that it was their task to drive "paganism" from the holy land undertook a holy war for that purpose. They are called *Zealots*, people zealous for the Lord. They led the later stages of the rebellion which began in 66 C.E. and culminated in the destruction of the Temple in 70. Some of them, who survived the fall of Jerusalem, retreated to Herod's castle at Masada, where they continued the struggle for nearly three years. At the end they committed suicide, rather than surrender to Rome.

Zikhronot: Remembrances, prayers on theme of God's remembering his mercy, covenant, in New Year Additional Service.

Zionism: Movement to secure Jewish state in Palestine, founded 1897 by Theodor Herzl.

Zohar: Medieval kabbalistic (= mystical) book, completed by fourteenth century in Spain; mystical commentary on biblical passages, stories of mystical life of the *tanna*, Simeon ben Yohai.

Biblical and Talmudic References

191

General Index